WINDOW BOX GARDENING

BY
ROY GENDERS

MAGNA PRINT BOOKS
PUDSEY YORKSHIRE

**First Published in large print 1974
by
Magna Print Books, Pudsey,
Yorkshire
by arrangement with
W. & G. Foyle Limited
London**

© **Large Print Edition 1974
Magna Print Books**

ISBN O 86009 0027

**Printed in Great Britain by
Redwood Burn Limited
Trowbridge & Esher**

CONTENTS

Chapter 1

THE CHARM OF WINDOW BOX GARDENING

The new gardening - Window box requirements - Planting schemes - Raising the plants.

Whilst the Englishman's love of gardening is as strong as ever, present-day economy has brought about a new style gardening. The continuous drift of the populations to the large industrial towns, where it is necessary to house the people in flats or small houses possessing little or no garden has brought about a new interest in gardening in miniature. Pot plants in the home, miniature gardens indoors, and the use of tubs and window boxes has almost revolutionized our gardening during the post-war years. The now almost prohibitive cost of the upkeep of the large country house and its grounds, and the necessity to devote as much time as possible to augmenting one's income, thus allowing only the minimum of time to devote to one's hobby, has brought about a demand for a house with as little garden as possible. The sunny window of a cottage has taken the place of the conservatory with its considerable demands on labour and heating, whilst the window box is replacing the large garden. But no matter how conditions might have changed, the Englishman's love of flowers remains as strong as ever. Time once spent on the herbaceous border and orchard is now used to beautify the home, whether a country cottage or town flat, by this new gardening in miniature. Yet so much more could be done to obtain greater satisfaction from the limited space at one's disposal.

WINDOW BOX REQUIREMENTS

All too often the window box is given little thought to its planting, with the result that the intended display will often prove disappointing. Not only is it necessary to use plants which by their size will prove suitable for window box culture, but it is even more necessary to ensure that the plants are tolerant of the conditions to which window boxes are exposed. This means a restricted root run and often a sun-baked position so that the plants must be capable of withstanding long periods with little or no protection from the hot summer sun. Quite often, too, the plants will be left unwatered whilst the holidays are taking place during summer. The length of time the plants are to be without attention, and conditions to which they will be exposed, must help to determine the type of plants which are to be grown. For example, all members of the geranium family will tolerate long periods without water, whilst another equally colourful window box plant, the multiflora begonia, demands copious amounts of moisture whilst in bloom.

A plant which may be classed as being really suitable for window box culture must be able to flourish with the minimum of attention. It must also be of compact, free flowering habit; whilst it must bloom over as long a period as possible. Again, the choice of plant will depend much on whether, if planted in a town, it is capable of withstanding the soot and sulphur deposits of town conditions. Certain plants are quite untroubled by such conditions, whilst others will fail to live up to reputations gained where planted under country or coastal conditions. Likewise, plants which grow well at the coast, where they are rarely troubled by frost, may prove disappointing where planted inland. All of which must be given careful consideration if the window box is to be appreciated to the full.

If only consideration was given to the very wide variety of plants for window box culture and their soil and climatic requirements , a far wider use could be made of window box gardening. Many of our factories, especially those which are not troubled by an excess of smoke, and town offices, could be made so much more attractive by the use of window boxes even if they grew nothing but the hardiest of evergreen plants. But primroses in spring, followed by the bright ornamental-leaf geraniums in summer and autumn would provide colour and interest with the very minimum of attention, whilst both plants remain quite untroubled by soot deposits.

Again, it is not necessary for the window box to be situated in full sun. There are numerous plants for a shaded and semi-shaded position where members of the primrose family and bulbs for spring flowering, followed by pansies and violas for summer, will prove most suitable. Even where the window box is exposed to strong winds, there are many suitable plants.

PLANTING SCHEMES

The window box may be filled with compost and planted either with plants in their season, or with permanent plants in the form of a miniature garden; or it may be used merely as a container to hold plants which are grown and flowered entirely in their pots. In this case it will not be necessary to fill the box with compost, though peat packed round the pots during summer will help to reduce artificial watering to a minimum. Nor will it be necessary to raise one's own plants to use in this way. Pots of cinerarias or hydrangeas to bloom during May and early June may be followed by zonal or ivy-leaf pelargoniums, to bloom from mid-June until September. The new dwarf pompon chrysanthemums in pots, may be used to provide autumn colour, to be followed by the hardy heathers to bloom through winter. Where it is required to raise one's own plants in pots, daffodils, double tulips and hyacinths may be raised in a dark cupboard or cellar, and may be brought into bud in a cool airy room for transferring to the window box in April. There they will bloom until June. The bulbs may then be replaced by geraniums which have been wintered in a frost-free room indoors and will be in bloom when transferred to the window boxes. Given the protection of a wall, the geraniums should not be troubled by frost until early November when the plants may be taken indoors again to be replaced with the winter-flowering heaths. These may be obtained from a nursery in November and will only require potting. If obtained with as much soil on the roots as possible, all they require will be some moist peat pressed round their roots in the pots. They will remain green and colourful until spring.

The same use may also be made of the window box where it is required to plant directly into the made-up box. There is no need to wait until summer to enjoy colour. Late in autumn, the boxes can be planted with suitable varieties of bulbs and primroses, to bloom from the New Year. Or wallflowers, retaining much of their foliage throughout winter, may be planted in November to bloom throughout late spring. They may then be followed by annuals which will either have been raised in one's greenhouse or frame, or will be purchased from a local nursery-man where plant hybridizers have catered for the new trend in gardening.

Until more recently, the choice of annual plants of suitable habit for window box culture was extremely limited. Such plants as the dwarf African marigold; the Tom Thumb antirrhinum; the Waldersee aster; dwarf petunias and the Red Hussar or Extra Dwarf Early Bird salvias were undreamed of in their compactness and freedom of flowering. Now the choice is immense, with plants for every situation and soil. There is no need to use the same plants year after year, possibly those plants, valuable as they are, which were used during the period between the two world wars to the exclusion of all others. Here, calceolarias and marguerites, petunias and pelargoniums come to mind. The garden lover, confined to his (or her) flat may now enjoy as wide a selection of plants as those grown in the open garden. No longer is it necessary to look upon the window box as being the Cinderella of gardening.

RAISING THE PLANTS

Though it is possible to obtain a wide variety of plants from local nurseries, or through the post, it must be said that a greater variety may be enjoyed, and one's window box gardening will take on additional interest where it is possible to raise one's own plants. It must not be thought that window box gardening may be enjoyed only where there is no garden. Could not the window box become an addition to the small garden, for it will not only add charm to the property, but will permit a wider interest to be taken in one's gardening activities. Even where the very smallest piece of ground is available, such as a yard surrounded by a small border, it may be used to transfer plants that bloom in spring, and where they may remain during the summer months, to be planted again in the boxes in November. Here, too, the seed of pansies and wallflowers may be sown and the plants transplanted for later use in the window box. A small frame will permit the autumn sowing and wintering of certain annuals and the growing of bulbs in pots to be transferred to the window box to extend the spring display. A frame will also be useful for hardening off those plants which may have been wintered indoors, or of annuals raised in a heated greenhouse. Where the window box can be enjoyed in conjunction with a small garden, greenhouse or frame, then it may be made to provide the very maximum amount of pleasure.

Nor is it always necessary to have the window box in front of a window. Here it may of course be enjoyed to the full from inside the room and if correctly made will greatly add to the aesthetic value of the property from outside, but not every window is suitable for a flower box. Many of those who live in blocks of flats, or in homes under the control of the local council, may not be permitted to fasten window boxes to the property. Also the property may be too exposed. Again the boxes be too difficult to maintain to be practical. Where there are difficulties, it may be possible to enjoy a window box on a small verandah, or fixed to the wall of a courtyard, where it may be sheltered and may be easily tended. A window box may also be made up as a miniature garden and placed inside the window, using plants which will thrive under such conditions.

The type of window box to be used will be governed by many factors. That requiring the minimum of trouble will be the plant container, constructed of painted wrought iron which will give a continental appearance to one's property. A window box of this type will not be suitable for filling with soil and so will be used entirely as a container for pot plants. Against the deep windows of a Georgian house, such a 'box' will be seen at its best, but would not be so happy if used with mullioned windows, or against the small windows of a country cottage. Here the the box made of wood, concrete or the period decorated fibre glass or plastic type would be superior, and the depth must be carefully considered. That to be used for a long, low window will need to be constructed less deeply than a box for a large, deep window . A shallow box provided for a large window would appear quite out of place and however attractively the box was filled this would not compensate for lack of proportion. Whether the container type box, or the more usual type of box is to be used, will depend upon what facilities there are for bringing on the young plants. Also upon whether one prefers the pleasures of making and tending a miniature garden rather than enjoying colour from pot plants with the minimum of trouble. But whichever method is preferred, some thought should be given to the most suitable plants which will provide colour the whole year round, and to the type of property before the boxes are made and the window box gardening commenced.

Where space for gardening is restricted, tubs or ornamental vases may be used to advantage placed on either side of an entrance to a house or courtyard and kept filled with flowering plants in much the same way as for window boxes. The tubs should be painted to match the window boxes and woodwork of the property.

CHAPTER 2
MAKING AND FILLING
THE WINDOW BOX

The need for care in fixing the window box - Measurements of the box - Making the box - Filling the boxes - Care of the box.

The plant rack or container in wrought iron will present no difficulties in its making, for it will have been purchased already made up to the size of the window. It will be held in place by brackets at both ends of the rack which should be painted black or white, the same as the rack. To make the container quite secure, the wall should be plugged with hardwood to a depth of not less than 2 in., into which the brackets are screwed. It is essential to see that there is no possible chance of the box protruding too far from the house, particularly where it is to overhang a public right of way, thereby causing injury to those who pass by, especially during hours of darkness. It is also equally important to ensure that neither the box nor its

contents are able to fall on those below, otherwise the owner may find
himself on the wrong side of the law.
So before the box is filled and planted
it must be fixed with the utmost care
and a professional joiner should be
called in for the purpose. It must be
remembered that on occasions a box
may be almost 4 ft. in length and 6 in.
in depth and so will contain a considerable quantity of soil. This will mean
that the supports will have to carry a
great weight especially when the soil
is wet. Any inefficiency in the filling of
the box will only lead to trouble, and
even if no harm is done, a box which
will break away from the walls when
in all its glory, will cause much disap-
pointment.

Where there is sufficient width to
place the box in position beneath a
window without the necessity of using
brackets, precaution must be taken
by fixing strong wire to the outer corners of the box. This is fastened to
hooks fixed in the wall on either side of
the window at a suitable position bet-

ween the stones or bricks. A box which may be placed on the flat top of a porch or door canopy and which may be tended from a window immediately above, should also be given additional support in the same way. It must be remembered that a window box in an exposed position will be subjected to strong winds and may also have to take a heavy weight of snow falling from the roof, so make certain that the box is thoroughly secure before it is filled.

The container of plants in pots will not be required to carry the same great weight as will say a concrete box filled with soil, and additional support for the latter should be made.

Another method, where the window frame and the box are made of wood, is to fix a 5 in. iron bracket along the top of the box and screw it into the window frame. It is, of course, necessary to have the box made to the exact measurements of the window, otherwise not only will it appear most unattractive, but will be difficult to fix correctly.

Take care, too, to ensure that the box is in such a position as to allow the window to open without difficulty, though this is not quite so important where the window opens up and down rather than outwards.

To support a concrete box, strong iron brackets should be securely fixed to the wall beneath the window and on these the box will rest. If the box is to be made more than 2ft. 6in. in length, then it should be given an additional support at the centre. The weight of the box filled with soil should hold it in position, but as an extra precaution, an eye screw should be fixed at the top of each side of the box as the concrete hardens. Through the eye, strong wire is placed and taken to a similar eye or staple fixed to the wall or window frame. If the wire is made quite tight, this will prevent any movement of the box, and if required it is quite an easy matter to remove the box at any time. Where the window is more than 3ft. 6in. in length, two separate boxes should be made and fixed separately alongside each other.

MEASUREMENTS OF THE BOX

In making the box, the exact measurements of the window must first be taken so that the sides of the box will coincide with the framework of the window. The depth of the box will be governed by the depth of the window. For a very deep window in factory or hotel, then the boxes may be 8in. to 9in. deep and this will allow a greater depth of soil so that the plants will require considerably less attention than where the boxes are less deep. For the windows of most town houses and where the house is of Georgian architecture, the boxes could be 6in. to 7in. deep; whilst for the generally long, low window of a medieval building or for the small, possibly mullioned window of a cottage, then the box should be about 5in. deep. The deeper the box the less attention it will require as to watering.

Distance from back to front is also important and this will be governed either by the construction of the window frame, where there may be quite a wide ledge; also by situation. Where there are low windows and the property is alongside a public footpath or highway, then the box must not unduly protrude. With many windows there is a ledge the width of a brick for a portion of the box to rest upon, and if the box is no more than 6in. from back to front, the slight protrusion will cause no trouble.

Where a row of plants in pots is to be used, then the window box or container need not be more than 5in. from back to front, but where the box is to be filled with soil, 6in. would prove more satisfactory and be of sufficient width to take a double row of plants. Where the window is large and there is no fear of protrusion, then the boxes may be 8 in. from back to front and of similar depth. This will permit the box to be in proper perspective with the size of the window. A large box will be able to accommodate the larger type of plant such as the hydrangea, pompon chrysanthemums and dwarf dahlias, whilst to the smaller box should be confined the most dwarf plants such as certain Juliae primroses, miniature bulbs and the more compact annuals such as the dwarf marigolds and the dwarf petunias.

There is little to be gained by using a concrete box rather than one constructed of wood. Though it may have rather a longer life, it will be much heavier and more difficult to construct and secure. A wooden box made of 1in. timber, treated with preservative and painted on the outside will prove long lasting and should present no difficulty in its construction and fixing. May I make one suggestion, and that is to use two boxes to maintain the display, one to fit inside the other. This will permit a far greater elasticity in the year-round display. For example, whilst the original box will continue with the summer display of annuals or geraniums right through autumn, these plants may be replaced by an inner box made up of bulbs and other winter flowering plants which will come into bloom as soon as placed in the permanent box, possibly in November. Or again, whilst the fixed box may be planted with plants and bulbs to bloom from Christmas until March, the second box will be planted to provide colour from April until early June. Yet another method is to allow the original spring display to continue until the end of May and then to replace with an inner box made up of annuals sown directly in the box in early April, possibly in a frame . There will thus be few periods when the window box will not be showing colour. The inner box, made of wood, may be fitted inside a fixed box constructed either of wood or of concrete. It is placed in by 'handles' of cord at either end and which are removed when the box is in position. A second box may be used in much the same way as where plants are grown in pots and brought on either in the home or in the greenhouse to maintain a succession of bloom. It is preferable that the inner or replacement box be of wood rather than of metal, for plants are never happy when their roots are in a non-porous container, however well drained it may be. For the same reason, a window box should be constructed either of concrete or of wood. These are porous materials and also possess a rough inner surface which is conducive to vigorous root action.

MAKING THE BOX

As a window box has to carry a considerable weight of soil, it should be constructed of 1in. wood, cut to the correct lengths and planed. The front and back of the box should be cut to the length required, the ends fitting inside. When cutting the ends, allow for the thickness of wood so as to keep to the correct overall measurements required. If any attempt is made to dovetail the corners it should be remembered that the strength of a dovetail lies in the perfection of its construction and a water-resistant glue should be used. Always bear in mind that a good, simple job is better than a bad complicated one. When securing the two ends no advantage will be gained by using screws instead of 2 in. nails, for when driven in they only tend to part the grain, thus splitting the wood. For additional strength at the corners an angle bracket should be screwed either on the inside or outside of the box.

Adequate drainage holes should be made in the base, preferably making a dozen or so holes of ½in. diameter rather than half the number of 1in. diameter, to ensure that there will be little of the compost escaping. Where possible always use hard wood such as seasoned oak, in the construction of the box, or failing that, American Red Cedar, both of which will remain almost impervious to moisture through the years and neither of which require painting as a preservative.

After the box has been made up it should be treated on the inside with a wood preservative, Cuprinol being most efficient. A lining of plastic film, with holes in it for drainage, prevents wood rot too. This treatment is especially necessary if the box has been constructed of deal or other soft wood. Thoroughly soak the inside of the box and allow it to remain in the open after treating for at least ten days until it has become thoroughly weathered and any fumes which might be injurious to plant life will have escaped. The box may then be painted on the outside only, to conform to one's tastes, or to the colour scheme of the house. The window box should be of the same colour as the window frames; turquoise, grey, or pale blue being most attractive, also cream or white. These shades seem to bring out the rich colours of the blooms to the utmost advantage. Against stone or mullioned windows then a box made of oak presents a better appearance if it is not painted. Filled with crimson geraniums the effect is extremely rich. Where the boxes are to be used against the white or cream washed walls of a cottage, a pleasing effect will be to paint the boxes and window frames pale blue or pink. Always use one of the more delicate colours, deep greens and brown never looking right for window boxes.

Owing to the weight of soil, the boxes are always fixed before they are filled, though it is preferable to add the drainage materials first. And always remember to place the boxes where they can be easily attended. To place them in some inaccessible position which necessitates the use of a pair of steps to give them attention, or where the watering-can has to be held at arm's length above one's head, will be to make window box gardening a toil rather than a pleasure.

It should be said that a box which is to be used inside the fixed box should be constructed of ¾in. wood to make its manipulation as easy as possible. An inner box, in which plants are already coming into bloom must of course be moved with the compost already in, and for this reason will be more easily used for those windows which may easily be reached from out-side.

The concrete box will be heavier and therefore should not be made more than 6in. deep, the base and sides being 1in., the same as for a wooden box. The concrete box, however, should be reinforced with wire netting.

The box is made from a wood mould, the sides being lightly held together so that they may easily be removed when the concrete has set. The base should not be nailed to the sides. The method is to mix the concrete, using 2 parts of sand to 1 part of cement, so that it is of such a texture as to pour without it being too thin or sloppy. The base is first made to a depth of 1in., corks at regular intervals being pressed into the concrete and removed when it has set. These are for the drainage holes. Then 1in. mesh wire netting is placed across the base before the concrete has set and this will also be used for reinforcing the sides.

When the base has partly hardened, an inner 'box' or mould containing no base is then placed inside, its dimensions being such that there will be a

1in. space between the sides of the two boxes. Into this the concrete is poured, the wire netting reinforcement being tacked to the top of the inner mould so that it will not show on the outside of the box when the cement has dried. This it will do in about twenty-four hours when the moulds are carefully removed and the wire netting reinforcement is trimmed level with the top of the sides. The box should be moved and the base prised off only when it it is thoroughly dry. It should then be weathered for at least a fortnight by allowing it to stand exposed to the elements, but not to frost which would cause it to disintegrate before it has set. Do not forget to insert the eye screws at the top of the sides, somewhere near the centre, before the concrete has set, so that they may be used for the wire supports. The boxes may be painted on the outside to match the paintwork of the window frames and to take away their unattractive appearance.

FILLING THE BOX

Before placing any compost in the boxes it will be necessary to ensure thorough drainage. First the drainage holes in the base must be made so that the soil does not fall through, and this is best done by placing a piece of fine mesh wire netting over the base. Then add a layer of crocks to a depth of about ½in. to ensure efficient drainage during winter. Over the crocks, a layer of turves placed grass downwards will occupy another 1½in. of the box. The remaining space, depending upon the depth of the box is filled with prepared compost.

The soil should preferably be taken from pasture, or be a good quality loam from a country garden and where the soil is not troubled by deposits of soot and sulphur. Soil taken from a town garden will generally be of an acid nature and will also contain a large number of weed seeds. Therefore pasture loam is greatly to be preferred. This should be stacked under cover when it is mixed with some peat and grit. A satisfactory compost will be made up by mixing

3 parts loam,

1 part peat,

1 part grit or coarse sand (by weight).

Allow 2lb. of ground limestone or lime rubble to a box 3ft. long and 6in. deep; 4oz. of bone meal, a slow-acting fertiliser and a sprinkling of super-phosphate which encourages a vigorous root action.

Whilst the same compost will not suit all plants a compromise may be made. For instance, geraniums prefer decayed manure to peat, whilst with begonias the reverse is the case. Most annuals, bulbs and spring-flowering plants will be happy where either peat or decayed manure is used, or half and half of each, which mixture would also prove acceptable both to begonias and geraniums.

It is important to make up a well-drained, friable compost, yet it must also be able to retain moisture during dry periods in summer. For this reason the peat or decayed manure, or a little of both, should not be omitted, and where the loam is of a light, sandy nature, then a larger proportion of humus materials should be added. It is important to keep the compost sweet as long as possible without the continual changing of the soil. Therefore lime in some form should not be omitted. A few pieces of charcoal in the soil will also help to maintain sweetness. Correctly prepared, the compost will not only make for healthy and vigorous plant growth, but will require changing only once every three years.

The window boxes, after they have been made quite secure, should be filled several days before they are to be planted so that the compost is allowed time to settle down. The compost is best taken to the boxes in a small bucket, and as it is placed in the box it should be pressed around the sides so that all air pockets will be eliminated. The box should be filled to the top and be allowed three or four days in which to settle down before any planting is

Window boxes and hanging basket can brighten up a drab frontage.

The Grape Hyacinth or Muscari

done. The compost will then sink to about ½in. below the top of the box which will allow for watering without the soil splashing over the side.

CARE OF THE BOXES

Planting will take place late in autumn for the spring flowering plants and bulbs, and again in early summer when the plants are replaced by those which bloom through summer and autumn. Where planting is to be done directly into the soil, pot grown plants should be knocked from the pots and taken to upstairs boxes in a clean wooden box, so that there will be the minimum of mess inside the house. Lower window boxes will be planted from outside. Plant firmly and allow the plants room to develop.

Where window boxes are being used as containers, the pots should be placed on a layer of peat which should also be pressed round the pots and kept comfortably moist to prevent undue evaporation of moisture in the pots.

The boxes should be given a dressing with lime each autumn as the plants are changed, and a small quantity of bone meal should also be worked into the soil which should be thoroughly stirred up. After three years the compost is best replaced and wooden boxes given another dressing on the inside with preservative. First remove the old compost, then take out the crocks which are replaced after the boxes have been treated. After ten days refill with freshly-prepared compost when, after it has had time to settle down, planting may be done.

Mention should be made here about watering the boxes. This will, of course, be determined by the weather, and for long periods it may not be necessary to water at all. Many plants, too, will withstand long periods without artificial watering. Where it is thought necessary to water the boxes give a thorough soaking to enable the moisture to reach right down to the roots so that they do not turn upwards in search of it. However, on no account give so much water that it will soak through the soil and drip from the bottom of the box. The boxes being situated under the eaves of a house and against the wall where they are shielded from the rains, they will tend to become dry even when the garden soil may be quite moist, so constant inspection of the compost should take place during the spring and summer.

Chapter 3
BULBS FOR THE WINDOW BOX

Methods of using bulbs in the window box - Care of the bulbs - Suitable composts - Allium - Babiana - Broadiaea - Chionodoxa - Corydalis augustifolia - Crocus - Eranthus - Erythronium - Galanthus - Hyacinth - Iris - Muscari - Narcissus - Scilla - Tulip.

The small flowering bulbs are amongst the most useful of all plants for a window box. They possess a neat, compact habit and if planted for succession will provide colour from early winter until the boxes are cleared to make way for the summer flowering plants early in June.

There are numerous ways of using these bulbs. They may be either potted, using 3in. pots and brought on in a cold frame after the usual period in the plunge bed and introduced to the window boxes as they come into bud; or the bulbs may be planted directly into the box. A second box for placing inside the fixed box may also be planted with the later flowering bulbs which may be brought on in a frame or in the open. They may then be introduced to the window position when coming into bloom early in May and will continue the display until the boxes are to be planted with summer flowering plants. When the bulbs are brought on in batches it will be necessary to have a frame or small piece of ground where they may remain from the time they leave the plunge bed until required.

When grown in pots, they should be inserted in peaty soil in the box, with the rims just beneath soil level. If brought on in a cold frame, or in a sheltered position outdoors, the plants in the pots or additional box may be showing leaf and bud when introduced to the window position. However, if grown in a plunge bed or in a darkened place in the home, they should be introduced to the box as soon as they commence to make growth. To grow them on in darkness would be for the plants to become 'drawn', and they would most probably be cut back by cold winds when planted in the boxes.

For those who live in the less favourable districts, possibly the best method, where a succession of colour is required over as long a period as possible, is to make up the boxes with bulbs in pots late in autumn, using those bulbs which are to come into bloom during the early winter months. These are then replaced early in May with bulbs which have been grown on in a cold frame, or in the open, in which case they will be introduced to the box when coming into bloom. These late bulbs should be followed by summer flowering annuals and plants of a less hardy nature, the begonias and geraniums, which are not generally planted out until mid-June.

Another idea is to plant up the box with winter and early spring flowering plants, such as primrose Barrowby Gem and winter-flowering pansies which are interplanted with pots of *Iris reticulata,* snowdrops, and other early bulbs. These will have almost finished flowering by the end of April when the boxes may be cleared entirely and refilled with double tulips growing in 60 size pots. Growing to a height of 9in. these will provide brilliant colour until replaced by geraniums or begonias, or plants of the late flowering annuals in early June. Where a window box can be combined with a small greenhouse, or even with a cold frame, the display may be greatly lengthened and the boxes enjoyed to the full. It should be the aim to have no colourless periods and in this respect bulbs are most accommodating.

Those who live in a flat, where it is not practical to bring on the bulbs other than in the window box itself, and where time for the attention of the boxes is at a minimum, there will be no alternative but to plant the boxes with a view to providing as long a display as possible. But rather than plant odd bulbs here and there, which would never give any worthwhile colour, they should be either planted directly into the soil of the box in groups of three or four, or should be set in small pots in the soil in similar numbers.

CARE OF THE BULBS

The bulbs may either be grown entirely by themselves, or they may be planted between flowering plants or miniature evergreen trees, which are also grown in pots so that they may be removed in summer without disturbing the roots. They may then be grown either on a balcony or in a sunny window, or may be planted in the open ground. Bulbs grown in pots may be removed immediately after flowering and others introduced without disturbing the rest of the box. The pots are then placed on their side in an airy, cool room - a garden shed or attic room will be suitable - to allow them to dry off and die back naturally. The bulbs are then shaken from the pots, cleaned of the soil and stored in boxes of dry peat until re-potted in autumn to be used again. Bulbs which have been planted directly into the boxes will be removed when the boxes are cleared to make way for the summer flowering plants. They should have the soil shaken from them and should be placed on sheets of paper in an airy room for the foliage to die down and the bulbs to dry off.

When planting the miniature flowering bulbs, do not set the bulbs too deeply. The smaller bulbs resent deep planting. A reliable guide is to cover them with the same depth of soil as the size of the bulb from top to base. In this way each is planted on its merits, not all being planted the same depth as is so often done.

SUITABLE COMPOSTS

Where growing in pots, place a small crock at the bottom before filling with a compost, made up of:-

2 parts soil,
1 part peat,
1 part sand or grit.

Where possible use fresh loam and when making up the compost add a small quantity of crushed charcoal to keep it sweet. The compost should be made up under cover so that it will be friable when used.

Early October is the best time to plant in pots, or at the month end where planting directly into the boxes. Those bulbs which are to come early into bloom should be set out in the boxes when they are made up during October and before the other winter and spring flowering plants are introduced so as to make as little disturbance as possible. The rims of the pots should be just covered with soil. Planting in this way will permit the compost of the boxes to be made up more to the requirements of the plants than the bulbs, and so all will receive the conditions they enjoy best. Where the bulbs are to be planted directly into the boxes, a compost as near as possible suitable to both plants and bulbs must be provided and here it is fortunate in that most of the winter and spring flowering plants, especially the pansies and primrose family, require much the same compost. This should be of a fresh loamy soil, enriched with a little decayed manure, some peat and a small amount of coarse sand or grit. To make up a window box 3ft. 6in. long, 9in. deep and 9in. wide will take a small barrowful of compost. The amount of peat should be about one-third by bulk, the rest being loam. To the whole is added half a bucket of decayed manure and the same amount of gritty sand. As an alternative to the manure, which may be difficult to obtain and handle in a town, work in 6oz. of bone meal. Mix the ingredients thoroughly, and add a small handful of charcoal. The window box must be well crocked to assist with winter drainage before adding the soil.

Where pots of bulbs are being grown on to bloom later, they must in no way be forced. For this reason they are best kept in a plunge bed away from the eaves of a house where dripping water might be troublesome. There the pots are covered to a depth of 4in. with soil, sand or ashes until thoroughly rooted. If the pots are plunged during October, rooting will have taken place by Christmas. From then onwards the pots may be either taken indoors and placed in a sunny window, or may be transferred to cold frames or a sheltered position outdoors, where they will grow on until required for the window box.

An efficient method is to make the plunge bed into a cold frame by surrounding it with 8in. boards. The plants are left entirely unprotected until the year end, when the pots are lifted and the cover soil is shaken off. They are then replaced in the frame which is then covered with a light. There the plants may remain until required for the window boxes and will continue to grow slowly. The following bulbs are suitable for window box culture:-

ALLIUM. Though most of the Flowering Onions are suitable only for naturalizing or for the border, *A. Ostrowskianum* bears its deep rosy-red heads early in summer on only 6in. stems. Where planting for successional flowering, where bloom is required until mid-June, bring on the bulbs in 2½in. pots in a frame and set them out in April.

BABIANA. This bulb is not quite hardy and so is best grown in pots in a cold frame for planting in the box in spring. The plants bear dark green hairy foliage, and throughout May, attractive blooms on 8in. stems, ranging in colour from blue to crimson.

BRODIAEA. The species suitable for a window box is *B. grandiflora* which bears pretty little bright blue flowers during May on 6in. stems. It is quite hardy but likes a position of full sun and a compost containing plenty of grit.

CHIONODOXA. All are very suitable for window box culture, in fact, there is no more brilliant flower for early spring. Unlike the crocus, they do not close up their blooms at the slightest cold wind, whilst they remain quite untroubled by sleet showers. Set the little bulbs six to a 3in. pot and plant 1in. deep. A pleasant idea is to set two or three bulbs of three species or varieties to a pot or pan, and so enjoy a long display of bloom of various colours. *C. sardensis* is the first to come into bloom early in March, when it bears on 4in. to 5in. stems, its loose sprays of rich gentian-blue flowers with their vivid white centre. Then at the end of the month blooms *C. Luciliae,* of similar habit, with its brilliant blue flowers and glistening white centres. Not without good reason is it called the Glory of the Snow. There is also a pure white form *C. Luciliae alba* and a rose-pink form *C. Luciliae rosea*; whilst the new Pink Giant, flowering on 6in. stems and bearing flowers of cyclamen-pink is enchanting. For April, *C. gigantea*, bearing its large lavender-blue flowers on 5in. stems, is very lovely. Planted with blue, purple or white winter-flowering pansies or with blue and white primroses, it is a delightful companion.

CORYDALIS AUGUSTIFOLIA. **This is a valuable little bulb for a shady window box. It grows well under town conditions and blooms best in a poorish soil, one containing plenty of sand or grit and only a little peat. It produces its pale lavender sprays on 8in. stems and remains in bloom from mid-March until the end of May.**

CROCUS. Both the large-flowered hybrids of Dutch origin and many of the species are very suitable for window box culture. Where the boxes are being planted with nothing but a succession of bulbs, then the autumn flowering crocus may also be used. The colchicum, which is generally known as the autumn crocus, as the flowers are similar, is not suitable for a window box as the foliage is too large.

The first of the Crocus species to bloom is *C. Imperati*, which produces its fawn and violet-scented blooms at Christmas and at the same time as primrose Barrowby Gem, rich yellow.

In bloom almost at the same time is *C. Zonatus* with its showy bloom of rose-lilac with an orange base. Then, whenever there is a milder day towards the end of January, *C. Fleischeri* is in bloom. Its striking small white flower with its orange-scarlet stigma is delightful in a window box planted with the wine coloured winter pansies. In February *C. Korolkowi*, with its vivid golden flowers comes into bloom. Then in March comes the handsome *C. Corsicus*, with its large bold flowers of deep cream and purple; and *C. susianus*, glossy gold and brown. At the same time the lovely *C. chrysanthus* varieties are also in bloom. E.A. Bowles, with its handsome canary-yellow flowers, is lovely; also the creamy-white Snow Bunting. In April *C. Thomasianus* opens its lovely sapphire-blue flowers. The new variety Taplow Ruby, wine-purple is quite outstanding. Even later to bloom is *C. Olivieri*, with its tubular blooms of brilliant orange-yellow, the last crocus to flower.

Of the Dutch or large-flowered hybrids, Vanguard comes early into bloom with its flowers of grey and mauve. Equally lovely is Queen of the Blues, silvery-purple; whilst Paulus Potter bears a huge bloom of ruby-purple. Plant as a companion, either the pure white Snowstorm, or Barr's Golden-Yellow. With each of these species and varieties, four bulbs should be planted to each pot, and where facilities permit, make a planting of those to bloom from Christmas until March, then replace with others to bloom during the latter weeks of spring.

The autumn-flowering species are not as suitable for a window box, for most bloom from September until early November when the summer flowering plants will still be colourful. However, where they may be planted in pots and brought on in a frame to be planted whilst in bud, those which bloom towards the end of November may be used, whilst one or two species which do not bloom until early December may be planted when the boxes are made up in autumn. Of these, *C. ochroleucus*, white with an orange base; the purple and buff *C. laevigatus* with its fragrant blooms; and *C. sativus*, the Saffron Crocus are really lovely species in bloom during December.

ERANTHUS. This, the Winter Aconite is an attractive plant for a small window box, though bearing its bloom on such short stems it is not conspicuous from outside. The most colourful variety is *E. Tubergeni,* a hybrid which bears very large golden-yellow blooms on rather longer stems and is in bloom during February and March.

ERYTHRONIUM. The Dog's Tooth Violet, so called because of the shape of the bulb and its dainty violet-like blooms, is not nearly so well known as it should be. This is a splendid plant for a shaded window box and in addition to its lovely flowers of purple, rose and white, which hover like butterflies on 4in. to 5in. stems, the glossy deep green leaves are attractively mottled. The plants will bloom during early spring and will provide an enchanting display together with the chionodoxa species. Plant in small pots, three bulbs to a 2½in. pot, and provide plenty of peat or leaf mould in the compost.

GALANTHUS. No winter window box would be complete without a few clusters of Snowdrops, their milky-white and green bells nodding in the wind. Not only are they early to bloom, but make a pleasing contrast to the more colourful bulbs and flowering plants. They should be planted in small pots, six bulbs to each, so that immediately after flowering they may be replaced by later flowering bulbs. One of the most attractive varieties is *G. Imperati Atkinsi,* which will bear its large snow-white tubes on 8in. stems soon after Christmas. At its best during February is *G. nivalis,* which is the familiar green-tipped snowdrop. The double form *flore plena* is rather later to bloom. For March flowering *G. Elwesii,* with its attractive grey foliage and large flowers with their vivid green inner segments held on 6in. to 7in.

stems, is an excellent variety.

HYACINTH. Quite a delightful display may be enjoyed by growing on the plants in a cold frame and transferring them in 3in. size pots to the window box when the spring display has ended. There they will bloom until early June, and whenever the window is opened will fill the room with their fragrance. Their thick fleshy flower spikes and long glossy dark green strap-like leaves make them an ideal window box plant, but they will require more attention to watering than most other bulbs, for they are copious drinkers. An attractive display may be obtained by planting the Double Daisies, especially Clibran's Mammoth Crimson with the white hyacinths. Of the white varieties, L'Innocence and Queen of the Whites bear a large spike; whilst by far the best red is Tubergen's Scarlet, which bears a massive blood-red spike with a striking crimson stem. L'Innocence and Tubergen's Scarlet bloom early and together. Where a real blue variety is required, Delft Blue and Grand Maitre bear a most handsome bloom; whilst Paul Veronese bears a refined spike of deep violet, lovely when planted with the salmon-pink Lady Derby or with the yellow varieties City of Haarlem and Yellow Hammer. Plant three top size bulbs to a 48 size pot, and after the usual period in the plunge-bed, grow on in a cold frame until ready for the window box. The flower spikes will need support which should be by special wire supports or by short canes and raffia.

The miniature blue Alpine Hyacinth is also a charming plant for a window box, bearing throughout May its dainty spikes of amethyst-blue. It grows only 6in. to 8in. tall.

IRIS. The dwarf irises are delightful plants for window box culture and are amongst the easiest of bulbs to grow. They all thrive in a soil containing some lime rubble and so are best grown in small pots in a compost enriched with this material and a small quantity of decayed manure in place of any peat. **Plant four or five bulbs to a 3in. pot which should be inserted into the box as they are made up in autumn, for these irises come into bloom very early in spring. Most attractive is** *I. Danfordiae* **which bears its bright golden blooms before the end of February. Then comes** *I. histrioides major,* **probably the best of all for a window box, for the quite large blooms are borne on 6in. to 8in. stems. The purple-blue flowers have a conspicuous white blotch on the fall petals.**

During March and early April *I. reticulata* **is in bloom, its sweetly fragrant flowers borne on 8in. to 9in. stems. The blooms are deep violet-purple with a striking yellow blotch on the fall. Possibly lovelier is Cantab, which has pale blue standards and rather deeper coloured fall petals which are attractively marked with a golden crest. As a companion, Royal Blue, which may be described as a pure Oxford blue colour, the fall petals having the same conspicuous golden blotch, is equally lovely. Each of the species should be**

planted in a sunny position and though the flowers have a rather frail appearance, they are capable of withstanding the most adverse weather.

MUSCARI. This is the grape hyacinth so called because of the hyacinth-like spikes of tiny rounded grape-like flowers. It is of the easiest culture and six bulbs should be planted to a 3in. pot. Planted amongst primroses or with yellow crocus or narcissus, they provide a most dainty effect and if several varieties are used they will give a continuous display from early March until May. The first to bloom is *M. azurem,* its spikes of bright Cambridge blue being borne on 6in. stems. Plant together the equally lovely pure white form, *album.* The well-known free-flowering hybrid Heavenly Blue, slightly taller growing and bearing its fragrant gentian-blue flowers throughout April, is equally attractive, and this is followed by the hybrid Cantab, of similar habit and bearing attractive pale blue flowers. The latest to bloom is *M. polyanthum* *album* which bears handsome spikes of pure white bells on 6in. stems, remaining more than a month in bloom.

NARCISSUS. Whilst for a deep window, almost all the large cupped daffodils will prove suitable for a window box, it is the miniatures that are most desirable. But first, the large-flowered varieties. These may be planted almost touching each other directly into the box to produce a massed effect of great beauty during April and May, but a better method is to plant four or five bulbs of the Large Round size to a 48 size pot (48 pots to the cast) and to bring these on in the plunge bed and cold frame ready to replace the early spring flowering bulbs and plants in April. The best varieties are those which bloom on 16in. to 18in. stems, varieties such as the tall growing King Alfred being less suitable. Possibly one of the finest is the large, deep yellow trumpet variety Magnificence. The trumpet is attractively serrated, whilst it is early to bloom. The variety Golden Harvest, its trumpet and perianth being deep golden yellow is also of sturdy habit. Those who like a white daffodil should plant the pure ivory-white Mount Hood which bears a bloom of great substance or Beersheba. And plant with it Dutch Master, a uniform soft yellow. Of the Jonquils, *N. odorus Orange Queen,* which bears three pretty, fragrant golden blooms to each stem, is compact and free flowering. Another lovely variety is Orange Queen, with deep golden orange scented flowers. The polyanthus narcissi are equally lovely, bearing three or four blooms to each stem. particularly attractive is Geranium with a pure white perianth and vivid scarlet cup.

The miniature narcissi are most charming in the small window box, or where the window is small, such as that of a cottage. Three bulbs should be planted to a 3in. pot and one of the loveliest varieties is February Gold, which grows to a height of 12in. and bears a lemon-yellow perianth with a frilled orange trumpet. It comes into bloom in March. Also a Cyclamineus hybrid is Beryl, which bears drooping globular flowers of orange-yellow on 8in. stems. Yet another is Peeping Tom which bears an elegant golden trumpet on a 15in. stem and remains long in bloom. Quite outstanding is *N. cernuus,* its silvery-white trumpets borne above blue foliage and on 9in. stems. Equally charming is a hybrid called Tete-a-Tete, which bears one or two flowers on 8in. stems, the blooms, with their reflexed perianth petals, being of a rich orange colour. Another worthy of note is Jack Snipe, which bears a pure white perianth and primrose trumpet. Unlike a number of the dwarf daffodils, each of these will bloom the first year.

SCILLA. It is *S. sibirica* which is useful for window box culture, *S. hispanica,* the Wood Hyacinth, growing too tall and making too much foliage. The best form of the Siberian Squill is the variety Spring Beauty which produces a succession of dainty spikes of a rich shade of purple-blue throughout spring and which makes this plant almost indispensable for a spring window box display. Plant four bulbs to a 3in. pot. For a later display *S. amethystina,* which bears its spikes of steely-blue on 8in. stems during May is also most showy and long lasting.

TULIP. All the single and double early tulips, with the exception of those which are of taller habit, will be suitable for window boxes. They will bloom from mid-April until mid-May and may be planted directly into the box in autumn or kept in a cold frame in pots until required to replace the early spring flowering plants. The double varieties with their very full blooms are more suitable for planting in pots for a late spring display. Most striking planted together is the new Scarlet Cardinal with Snow Queen, or the turkey red Carlton with the salmon and yellow Marechal Niel. Of the singles, Pink Beauty, the crimson-red Brilliant Star, the pure whites Diana and White Hawk, the yellow and orange Sunburst and the deep rose Ibis all bloom on 12in. stems.

The Kaufmanniana tulips which come early into bloom and bear their large brilliantly coloured flowers on 8in. to 10in. stems are ideal window box plants. One of the earliest is The First, its bloom having a carmine exterior and golden centre and measuring 6in. across. Very distinct is Shakespeare with its bloom of salmon and orange, whilst *K. aurea,* the outside of the petals brilliant scarlet, the inside bright yellow, is also outstanding.

A strain of Kaufmanniana hybrids, with mottled foliage and with the blooms even larger, would appear to be ideal window box subjects. Striking is Mendelssohn, the exterior of the petals being rose-red; the centre being splashed with spots of red.

Chapter 4

THE WINDOW BOX DURING WINTER AND SPRING

To provide colour during a dull period -

Bellis - Erica - Myosotis - Polyanthus - Primrose - Saxifrage - Wallflowers - Winter-flowering Pansy.

At no other time of the year is colour in the window box more appreciated than during the latter weeks of winter and throughout springtime. During the first weeks of the New Year when the colour and excitement of the Festive Season has passed, with the weather bleak and the sky overcast, any particle of colour will be greatly appreciated. From outdoors the appearance of a house will at this time of the year be considerably enlivened with colourful plants, whilst from inside, to gaze upon plants in bloom will be to bring a breath of spring to what is generally so dull a time of the year. And it is surprising just how many delightful flowering plants there are for winter and spring. Bulbs alone will provide colour, but few really open their blooms during the bleakest days, whilst if used with suitable flowering plants the period of blooming will be both extended and made more

A window box full of hyacinths

Here is one of the dainty miniature daf-fodils—Triandrus alba, Angel's Tears

interesting. What is more, with those plants which appreciate cool conditions, it matters little whether they are to be grown in a north, south, east or west position, though they will come earlier into bloom where they receive at least a little sunshine.

To provide a 'frame' for the flowering plants, variegated ivy, Hedera Silver Queen, with its neat grey-green leaves, attractively edged with silver, should be planted at the front or sides of the box. Or two may be planted around a tub. Insert the plant, still in its pot (for ivies hate root disturbance) beneath soil level so that when the box is being refilled and cleaned, the ivy may be removed and replanted with the minimum of disturbance. Over the front of the box the dainty fronds will trail and will be continually evergreen. Or plant at either end of the box and allow the plants to trail across the box and around the window.

Or plant the variegated periwinkle, *Vinca minor variegata,* with its silvery-grey evergreen foliage as a background for the bulbs and flowering plants; or one or two of the miniature shrubs, which must of course be ever-green. In this way the window box is built up to look like a garden in minia-ture rather than just a row of plants.

BELLIS. Double Daisies, *Bellis perennis,* which bloom during late spring and early summer and remain compact and tidy, are quite charming used entirely by themselves, or they can be planted with primroses and bulbs. The very dwarf varieties such as Dresden China will be best in the trough garden or where a miniature rockery is to be made in a window box. Of the more robust varieties, produc-ing double flowers as large as a ten-penny piece on 6in. stems, the crimson Etna and the pure white Snowball, both of which come reasonably true from seed sown in May, are striking when planted together. Longfellow is also pleasing, with its quilled petals of deep pink, and is particularly attractive with forget-me-nots.

ERICA. The flowering heathers are

not good mixers, and almost all of them require a lime-free, acid soil. There is, however, one class, the *Erica carnea* group, which will flourish in any ordinary garden soil and which bloom through the severest of winters. They are seen at their best either when planted together so that they will provide a succession of colour, or with the charming dwarf winter Jasmine, *J. parkeri* with its tiny bells of golden-yellow.

The value of *E. carnea* is its extreme hardiness, the plants being lifted late in October and planted in the boxes almost touching each other. Bushy plants from the specialist growers will often cover an area of 9in. to 10in. square, and they may be used almost indefinitely if removed from the boxes and transferred to peaty soil in April. This would allow seeds of annual plants for summer flowering to be sown at the correct time. Not all the winter-flowering heathers come into bloom at the same time. First are the lovely shell-pink varieties James Backhouse and Pink Pearl, both of which bloom from mid-November until mid-January, when the excellent Springwood heathers, pink and white, take over. These are splendid varieties for a window box, being extremely compact and they remain in bloom until early March.

Flowering from early December until early March, the crimson flowered King George V provides a striking contrast to the paler colours and is a most warm colour for winter. In bloom at the same time is the dark pink Winter Beauty. The last to bloom is the bright red Ruby Glow which comes into bloom mid-February and remains colourful until early April; and *E. vivelli,* of compact habit and which bears deep carmine-pink flowers.

These hardy ericas are propagated either by division of the roots after flowering, or by rooting cuttings. These should be taken in April and inserted 2in. apart in a peaty soil in a partially shaded position. Or they may be rooted in boxes of soil, peat and sand. The cuttings must be kept moist throughout summer.

MYOSOTIS.   Blue Ball is the most suitable forget-me-not for a window box, for it makes a ball-like plant no more than 6in. high, the blooms being of a rich indigo-blue colour. *M. Wraysbury blue* is slightly taller growing, but very striking where planted with yellow tulips or daffodils. The large flowers are of a bright steely-blue with a yellow centre, whilst each bloom has twice the usual number of petals. The special dwarf strain of Sutton's Royal Blue and Carmine King, both growing to a height of only 7in. to 8in., are also suitable.

Seed is sown in boxes or in the open ground early in summer. If the seed is thinly sown in the open, no transplanting will be necessary until the plants are moved to the boxes in late autumn. If sowing in boxes, transfer the seedlings, as soon as large enough, to deeper boxes containing soil which has been enriched with peat or leaf mould. Forget-me-nots like a moist, friable soil

Those who may wish to 'edge' their boxes will find Myosotis Sutton's Miniature, with its bright blue flowers borne on tiny rounded plants only 3in. to 4in. tall, quite delightful. The box could then be filled with red tulips or the taller and later flowering polyanthus. The dwarf Golden Bedder wallflower could also be used.

POLYANTHUS. Members of the polyanthus family, especially the miniatures are delightful plants for a window box, and quite the best strain ever grown by the author is the Barnhaven polyanthus-primroses from Oregon. The large flower heads are borne on sturdy 6in. to 8in. stems and they take in every conceivable colour, from dusky grey to terracotta, from shell pink to wine red. The usual white, yellow and cerise shades with which we are all too familiar, have been entirely eliminated. The same strain of Blue Primroses and Polyanthus is equally fine, the colour being fixed, the nearest to sky blue yet to appear in this plant. The blue primroses are at their best planted amongst yellow double tulips or daffodils. Of named varieties of blue primroses Cecily Mordaunt, dark blue with an inner ring of crimson; Sir Lancelot, a blue Garryarde; and Blue Horizon, a 'sport' of the well-known Wanda, are all attractive.

Of the miniature polyanthus, Lady Greer with its masses of tiny pale yellow blooms and Miss Osborne, deep mauve, are altogether charming plants.

Growers of the primrose family in towns frequently experience loss of buds through sparrows, and it may be advisable to place black thread over the plants early in spring. This would not be noticeable either from the house or from outside.

PRIMROSE. In bloom at the same time, that is, right through winter and spring, is the polyanthus-primrose Barrowby Gem which carries a delightful perfume. The clear yellow blooms are held on 6in. stems. Another of this valuable family is the variety Hunter's

Moon, in bloom from September until June, the bloom being of a luminous apricot colour and possessing almost as strong a fragrance as Ena Harkness rose.

Like all the primula family, the plants are extremely hardy and will withstand the bleakest situation but unless kept moist during summer they are best lifted towards the end of May and planted in a shady corner of the garden. They may be transferred to pots or deep boxes if there is no garden, and there they may remain throughout summer in a soil containing plenty of peat and kept continually moist. Protected from the summer sun and never lacking moisture the plant will multiply and may be divided when replanted in late autumn.

Most of the hardy Juliae primroses, of which Wanda is perhaps the best known, are also excellent, but unless the winter is particularly mild they will not come into bloom until the milder days of March, depending upon the district. But they are well worth waiting for, remaining in bloom until the end of May and being literally smothered in blossom. The plants are of two forms, those of upright habit, growing to a height of about 6in.; and those of cushion-like habit, making little foliage and with the blooms borne on stems only 1in. in length. It is the former which are more suitable for window boxes. The latter are ideal for trough gardens, for their colour and beauty would not be conspicuous used in a window box.

Those of taller habit include the striking Perle von Bottrop, with bloom of a bright shade of velvet-purple; Tawny Port, having maroon foliage and bloom of a dusky port-wine colour; Anita, its bright navy-blue flowers held well above its foliage; Dorothy, its pale lemon-yellow blooms having attractively waved petals; and the lovely Garryarde primroses with their bronze tinted foliage of which Guinevere, dusky pink and Hillhouse Red, crimson are outstanding.

Charming too are the hose-in-hose

primroses, well-known to Tudor gardeners, one dainty flower growing from another. Brimstone is lovely with its blooms of pale yellow held on 6in. stems. Plant with it the striking Irish Sparkler, its orange-scarlet blooms with their bright golden centre being held on 8in. stems. Nor must the free flowering Lady Lettice be omitted; its apricot, salmon and yellow blooms have a fairylike daintiness whilst they come early into bloom. The rosy-mauve Lady Molly is also lovely.

Whilst many of the old-fashioned auriculas, later to come into bloom than the primroses, are rather too tall for a window box, particularly the Dusty Millers, several are most suitable. One of the best is Blue Velvet with its heads of velvety-purple, the bloom having a striking white centre; whilst the lemon coloured Celtic King with its attractive waved petals and delicious fragrance is also excellent. The hardy auriculas cannot be said to be as easy to manage in a window box as the primroses owing to their woody root stock, the primroses being more fibrous rooted. They are best kept in pots which should be inserted into the box in winter and removed towards the end of May to spend the summer months in shade.

Of the other members of the large primula family suitable for window box culture, *P. capitata* bears its rich purple ball-like flowers on 6in. stems during early spring, whilst *P. denticulata* bears its ball-shaped heads on 9in. to 10in. stems. The variety *alba,* white, is rather too tall for a window box, but Rose Bengal, with its blooms of dusky pink and the deep purple-red Hay's Variety are ideal. They should be planted close together and entirely on their own for their leaves are large and upright. They are ideal plants for a shaded position, when they will come into bloom in early March and remain colourful until early May. They may be planted with large-flowered daffodils to continue the display until early summer.

SAXIFRAGE. Planted with the less

robust plants, several of the Kabschia or Cushion Saxifrages are delightful subjects. They like a gritty soil, containing plenty of leaf mould or peat, and so are best planted with dwarf primroses and the less robust bellis, such as Rob Roy. They are suitable plants for a window box alpine garden, planted so that they will provide colour throughout the year, and where they may remain in position. Or they may be grown in pots and inserted amongst the primroses, bulbs and Double Daisies in early spring.

Lovely is *S. Grisebachii* Wisley Variety, which forms silver rosettes and stems during early spring. Also suitable is *S. Frederici Augusti* with silvery foliage and bearing arching spikes of pink flowers on 6in. to 7in. stems. The true Cushion varieties, growing to a height of 2in. or less, are best used in the trough garden.

WALLFLOWERS. Wallflowers tend to make rather bushy plants even though certain varieties do not grow tall. For this reason it is advisable to grow them with forget-me-nots to the exclusion of the other perennials. In this case, several plants of the very beautiful dwarf yellow variety, Golden Bedder, planted closely together, would produce a mass of bloom if edged with myosotis, Sutton's Miniature. Plants of Golden Bedder grow only 8in. tall, whilst the Dwarf Mixed Bedding strain is even more compact.

Wallflowers have the advantage of remaining green through winter, whereas primroses tend to die back and show little foliage until the fresh bright green leaves appear in March. But whereas primroses are extremely hardy in the most exposed positions, wallflowers and myosotis may be troubled by cold winds and severe frosts when the plants are often badly damaged. Again, plants in a town window box, especially in an industrial area, will collect deposits of soot and will be anything but green-looking by spring, though this should be partly hidden when they come into bloom.

With a winter and spring window

box, where the plants will generally be planted in late autumn, consideration should be given to aspect and situation. In a bleak position facing north, the hardy pansies and primroses would be a suitable choice, planted with bulbs and the Double Daisies. Where winter colour is desired, then the Winter pansies and primroses Barrowby Gem and Hunter's Moon should be planted. Those who would prefer to enjoy the rich fragrance and vivid colour of the wallflowers in May and whose window boxes are in any way exposed, may overcome the difficulty by withholding planting until early spring, though it will be necessary to reserve one's plants at the nursery in the autumn. Where growing one's own wallflowers allow them as long a period as possible in which to build up a sturdy plant. Victorian gardeners would transplant at least four times, generally over a slate bed to prevent the formation of tap roots. Though this may not be practical today, the seed should be sown as early as April and as thinly as possible. Transplant the seedlings as soon as large enough to handle and keep them growing on by never allowing them to become dry at the roots. A plant that has become quite bushy by winter will be better able to withstand adverse conditions.

Wallflowers should not be grown where it is desired to plant hardy annuals in the window box or where the annuals are to be sown directly into the box, for it will be early June before the wallflowers finish blooming. Follow with geraniums, or begonias, or with the less hardy annuals such as petunias, which are not generally planted until the second week of June. Though hardy perennials, both wallflowers and forget-me-nots should be treated as biennials and destroyed after flowering.

WINTER FLOWERING PANSY. This is one of the most valu-able flowering plants which is not nearly so widely planted as it should be. If necessary, the plants will remain compact and provide colour all the year round and for at least two years if any unduly long shoots are removed early in summer. Or strong plants may be planted late in autumn when the box is made up and removed after blooming in early June to make way for the summer flowering plants. It is suggested that a window box should be made more permanent than is generally so, by using winter, spring and summer flowering plants together so that there will be continuous colour with the very minimum of trouble and expense. It must be remembered, however, that all the plants used for winter and spring display are perennial, and unless there is space available in the garden, however small, in which to transfer the plants when they have finished blooming in May, they should be made permanent and used with summer flowering annuals or foliage plants.

The winter pansy will bear at least some bloom during the very coldest of winter days. Particularly hardy are the yellow and white varieties whose bloom is also the most brilliant. Planted with trailing ivy, or with miniature trees or shrubs, these plants will provide a boxful of colour from Christmas until June, when they may be cut back and will come into bloom again a month or so later. But for the plants to bloom in profusion it is necessary to sow seed in April. A small packet of mixed seed sown in a seed pan in a sunny window, the seedlings being pricked off into small pots or boxes in which they are grown on during summer, will make sturdy, bushy plants capable of withstanding the most severe weather and blooming from early winter onwards.

One of the most colourful varieties is Winter Sun, the golden-yellow blooms having a black centre, whilst Helios is entirely without. Bearing a larger bloom of brightest gold is the new Orion; whilst North Pole bears a bloom of pure white. These two are perhaps the hardiest of all.

A most attractive variety is the dark velvety blue, March Beauty. Blue Boy bears a bloom of silvery-lilac; whilst there is also the attractive Wine Red. Several planted together make a glorious display.

Plants growing in a window box during winter and spring should need no watering except perhaps where growing in a position of full sun, when occasional watering may be necessary during the month of May. Dead blooms of primroses and violas should be removed as they form so that their already long flowering season will be even more prolonged.

Chapter 5
THE WINDOW BOX IN SUMMER

Suitable plants, their use and culture — Plants for summer flowering — Begonia — Calceolaria — Cineraria — Heliotrope — Marguerite — Salvia — Plants for autumn flowering — Chrysanthemum — Michaelmas Daisy.

THE basis of the window box in summer and autumn will be those valuable long flowering plants so popular for summer bedding, e.g. geraniums, marguerites and salvias. For window box display they are able to withstand the weather of an English summer which frequently alternates between periods of sunshine and conditions of drought, and long sunless periods often accompanied by heavy rains.

During summer, the window box may act as a container for plants grown in pots, or the boxes may be made up with suitable compost and the plants set out just as for bedding. With the exception of the Geranium family, which is the most important of all window box plants, and for this reason must be given a chapter to itself, each of the plants used for summer display must be grown in a warm greenhouse or sun-room, or must be obtained from a specialist grower when the boxes are being made up in June. The geranium is so valuable in that once the plants have been obtained, they may be wintered in the window of a living room, requiring no more heat than to keep the room free of frost.

There they may be propagated, whilst the original plants may be used again and again.

Other popular summer flowering plants are valuable in that they are so colourful and are so long flowering, and for these reasons they should not be neglected. A colourful combination to use is scarlet salvias with marguerites; the multiflora begonias with the silver leaf leucophyta. Scarlet geraniums and yellow calceolarias may also be grown together. The value of all these plants is that they may be brought into bloom indoors and will be colourful from the moment they are planted in the boxes. This is where these plants have an advantage over the annuals, but whether the plants are to be grown in their pots or are to be planted into the compost of the boxes will depend upon which plants are to be used for the spring display. Cinerarias, grown in pots and placed in the window box towards the end of May, will provide rich colour until the end of June. They may then be replaced by geraniums or salvias, which in turn may be replaced by the dwarf Michaelmas daisies and chrysanthemums grown in pots and which will remain in bloom until the end of November. This will mean that the boxes will need to be planted with care for winter and spring flowering. It will perhaps be better to concentrate on the late winter and early spring display so that the boxes can be cleared by mid-May to take the cinerarias, and in favourable districts any of the other summer flowering plants. In this way, the boxes should be planted with the hardiest of the primroses, winter flowering pansies and the early flowering bulbs so that they can be cleared early. If it is desired to use tulips or daffodils, wallflowers and the later flowering primroses and polyanthuses, then the boxes cannot be made up with the summer flowering plants until mid-June. Grown in pots they will, however, be in no way troubled by the delay in planting.

Some thought should also be given

to the material of which the house is constructed before making the selection of plants, and the attention the boxes can be given during summer should also be considered. Geraniums, marguerites and calceolarias are able to withstand quite long periods without moisture, whereas begonias and salvias require to be kept continually moist. In colours, scarlet flowers are at their best against a grey stone wall or a whitewashed house, whilst yellow and white flowers are seen to advantage against brick.

PLANTS FOR SUMMER FLOWERING

BEGONIA. It is the multiflora begonia rather than the large flowering type which is so valuable for window box culture. The plants are raised either in boxes or in small pots to be planted into the compost of the window box either when in full bloom or after they have been started into growth. This will depend upon when the tubers were planted; a warm greenhouse permitting an early start.

The small tubers should be started into growth about the last day of March and they will grow in a cold house or frame, though but slowly, and it will be July before they come into bloom. With gentle heat they will be ready for planting out in early June and will come into bloom by the middle of the month. The compost for starting the tubers into growth should consist of fibrous turf loam to which has been added some peat and coarse sand in the ratio of 2 parts turf to 1 part each peat and sand. Begonias like some lime added to the soil, and to each bushel of compost add 1½oz. superphosphate and ¾oz. lime. The tubers may be started in boxes, being merely pressed into the compost, and for the first weeks until they commence to make growth will require little water. When they are making growth they will prove to be copious drinkers.

This same demand for moisture will continue through summer, and if the plants are to be set out in a light sandy soil it must be fortified with farmyard manure, peat, spent hops or any similar form of humus. A heavy soil, which is preferable provided it is well drained, should be opened up by adding some grit and some peat. But above all, some lime is essential, for begonias are never happy in the acid soils of our cities. A 2oz. per square yard dressing with bone meal will provide food over the entire summer months.

The plants should be set out about June 7th/8th, when all fear of frost has gone. Plant 6in. apart, pressing the tubers 3in. below the soil surface and taking care not to break the brittle stem. From the time the plants are set out they must be watered copiously and should be given a mulch of peat in late July to conserve soil moisture through the summer. All dead blooms should be removed as they form so that they will not set seed, but this is not necessary with the multifloras. At their best in a season of damp, humid days, when other plants such as geraniums and calceolarias look anything but happy, begonias are particularly suited to our English climate in spite of their South American origin.

Lifting and storing begonias calls for care. The plants should be lifted with only their foliage and blooms removed, the stems being intact so that they can be placed in a frostproof room, dry and well ventilated, and there be left to die down gradually. Care must be taken in the same way with lifting as in planting, so that the stems are not broken. If the plants are lifted at the beginning of October, the stems will come away naturally from the tubers by the month end. The tubers should then be placed in boxes of dry peat, where they will remain through winter.

As the tubers become older they will increase in size and if not divided will tend to die back. The best method is to divide those large tubers when they have commenced growth in spring, for it is necessary for each piece to contain a shoot. The cut portions should be dusted with sulphur or charcoal to help the cut to heal over. Or the stock may be increased by taking cuttings as the young shoots appear in spring, generally a single shoot from an over-crowded tuber being removed. Side shoots may also be removed when 3in. to 4in. long as they appear on the main stems. Take care not to damage the 'eye' which will be seen at the base of each shoot and which must be removed with it.

The shoots are placed round the sides of a 60 pot containing a mixture of sand and peat, in the same way as with geraniums, and if kept moist will root in from three to four weeks. The best time to take cuttings is during June and July; if taken later they may not root too readily. The rooted plants should be potted into small pots con-taining a compost made up of loam, decayed manure, together with a little peat and some grit.

Of the Multifloras, Rambouillet, each plant covering itself in masses of flame red blossoms; Flamboyant, cherry-red; Madame Richard Galle, orange; and Madame Helen Harms, double yellow, are excellent varieties for a window box, making round compact plants 8in. to 9in. in height and remaining perpetually in bloom.

CALCEOLARIA. On account of the rich colouring of its blooms which are continuously borne until autumn, this is an excellent plant for a window box used with salvias or scarlet geraniums. Golden Gem and Bronze Beauty are the two best calceolarias for a window box.

The best time to take cuttings is in September, and only those shoots which have not borne a flower should be removed. Firm side shoots should be selected and these should be inserted into boxes containing a mixture of peat and sand. If kept in a temperature of 60° F. they will root in several weeks, but take longer to root than most plants, for the shoots are hard and shrub-like. Early in spring, when well rooted, the plants should be transferred to 3in. pots containing the same materials as for salvias, and from then onwards should be given the same treatment. As the cuttings show a tendency to damp off, powdered charcoal should be scattered over the compost, and they should be kept dusted with sulphur whilst rooting.

CINERARIA. For early summer flowering, used as an alternative to tulips and primroses, and to bridge the gap between the winter flowering plants and those which come into bloom late in June, cinerarias grown in 3in. pots are charming plants for a window box. They should, however, be given a sunny, yet sheltered position, for the large heads of bloom may be damaged by strong winds and rain where too exposed.

Strains deserving attention for window box culture on account of their dwarf, compact habit and the individual blooms being placed close together enabling them to withstand adverse weather so much better are the Hansa Strain with small, neat foliage and a wide range of bright colours; Triumph mixed, Gublers Double mixed and Gaytime mixture.

Cinerarias require cool conditions in their raising. The seed should be sown as near July 1st as possible in boxes of sterilized soil containing a little sharp sand, barely covering them, and placed in a moist-shaded frame. Take care to see that on no account does the soil become dry, and as the seed germinates quickly under correct conditions — a little light must be admitted as soon as the seedlings appear. Ventilate freely so as to keep the tiny plants as strong as possible, and as soon as large enough to handle prick out into boxes of prepared soil, 2in. apart. From then onwards, keep the soil moist, give plenty of air and keep the plants shielded from bright sunlight, for it will then be the height of the summer and any carelessness in this respect will be fatal. Under suitable conditions the plants will soon be ready to move into 3in. pots. These should be either new or have been well scrubbed and filled with a not too rich but not too impoverished compost.

After three or four weeks they will be ready for a final move into the 5in. size. When once established in this size, water freely, for cinerarias are big drinkers. Spray with quassia solution every third week and with clean water every warm day. When the frost appears in mid-October remove the plants to a warm greenhouse where they remain over winter and come into bloom early in May. They should be placed in the window boxes towards the middle of the month.

HELIOTROPE. The old-fashioned heliotrope is an attractive window box plant, used with pink geraniums, with fuchsias, or with *Cineraria maritima.* Like the begonia, the plants prefer a sunny position and a compost which will retain summer moisture.

Propagation is from cuttings taken from stock plants in early summer for using in the window boxes the following year. The plants, however, may be wintered in a sunny room which is free from frost.

Rooted in sand, to which has been

added a sprinkling of peat to retain moisture, the cuttings may take eight to ten weeks to form roots, but will be speeded up if dipped in hormone powder. The cuttings are moved to small pots as soon as rooted and are transferred to 3in. pots during summer. The plants are kept almost dry throughout winter and in spring are brought on for bedding out early in June after being hardened in the usual way.

Heliotrope may also be raised from seed sown in a warm greenhouse during August. The seedlings are pricked out into small pots when large enough to handle and are grown on through winter as dry as possible. Started into growth again in spring, they may be large enough for outside bedding by early summer or could be repotted into 60's, placed in a frame over summer and used for bedding the following year. The Regal Hybrids bear large trusses of fragrant blooms in shades of purple and mauve and are suitable both for bedding and as a pot plant.

MARGUERITE. Because of their

rather informal habit, they were at one time planted with geraniums and calceolarias; their whiteness, long lasting qualities, and their ability to flourish under all conditions, made them a perfect foil to the brilliant colours and stiff habit of their neighbours. The plant may be classed as almost hardy, yet to propagate, the cuttings should be struck in gentle heat. October is the best time to remove the shoots from the leaf joints, when the plants are being removed from the beds. They are inserted in a compost of loam, peat and sand and kept in a temperature of 55° F., spraying occasionally to prevent flagging. As soon as rooted, the plants should be potted into 3in. pots in a compost containing some decayed manure and some grit. Like the geranium, the plants should be given very little water until the sun's rays stimulate growth towards the end of March. During April, as with all these half-hardy plants, heat will only be necessary at night; and from May 1st not at all. Early in May the plants should be moved to cold frames and hardened off in the normal way for planting in the boxes early in June.

SALVIA. Though quite easily raised from seed provided a temperature of 70º F. can be maintained until germination (an expensive method), salvias for window box culture, that is the dwarf scarlet *Salvia splendens,* are more profitably increased from cuttings taken in autumn. The cuttings, which should be about 3in. long, are inserted in boxes or around the rim of a pot in exactly the same way as geraniums, or the bedding plants may be lifted in late October, transferred to pots or boxes, and if kept in gentle heat, will continue to bear cuttings during winter. These may be removed and rooted in batches as they form. They should be kept in a temperature of 55º F., syringing them frequently to guard against red spider. As soon as rooted they are transferred to 3in. pots. The salvia is a gross feeder and must be given a compost containing a stiff fibrous loam, decayed manure, a little grit to keep the compost 'open', and a small quantity of bone meal. To keep the habit compact, the plants should be firmly potted. They should be transferred to cold frames for hardening about mid-May and given copious amounts of water. They should also never lack moisture when in the window boxes, to which they are removed early in June, planting them 6in. to 7in. apart.

The variety Scarlet Pigmy, which grows to a height of only 6in. to 7in., is an ideal bedding plant for a window box. Of the others, growing to a height of 15in., Harbinger, vivid scarlet, is long in bloom; Blaze of Fire, scarlet-crimson, is early and rather more compact.

PLANTS TO BLOOM IN AUTUMN

CHRYSANTHEMUM. Grown on through the summer months in 3½in. pots, the Dwarf Lilliput chrysanthemums provide rich colour to take over from the summer-flowering plants for flowering during autumn. Provided there is a sunny courtyard in which to bring on the plants during summer, it is not necessary to have a garden for their culture. Rooted plants may be purchased in early April thoroughly hardened and which will be ready to pot into 60 size pots. If placed in deep boxes of peat which is kept moist through summer there will be less evaporation of moisture from the compost in the pots. Propagation is from cuttings or rooted pull-offs which are taken when the plants are removed in November, and grown on under glass. Alternatively, the plants may remain in their pots undisturbed until spring, when rooted offsets are removed and grown on in pots.

This race of miniature chrysanthemums make bushy, compact plants growing only 9in. to 10in. in height and almost as wide. So free flowering are they that individual plants have been known to bear more than 500 blooms in a single season. One of the best is Honeybird, its pompon-like blooms being of a rich shade of orange-rust. Equally fine is Redbreast, the bloom being of vivid scarlet-crimson. Lovely for planting with the dwarf Michaelmas daisies is Horus, pale shell-pink and Isis, deep rose-pink. Where a yellow is required, Happy blooms early in autumn; Tom Tit is very late.

MICHAELMAS DAISY. Several of the dwarf asters growing to a height of only 9in. to 10in. are ideal plants for window box culture, for like the Lilliput Chrysanthemums they form neat, compact bushes and bear a profusion of bloom throughout autumn. Plants may be grown on in the open ground when they may be lifted into 5in. pots as they come into bud. Propagation is by division immediately after flowering. Outstanding varieties are Lady in Blue, the plants being smothered in semi-double bloom of deep blue; Queen of Sheba, lilac-pink; Rose Bonnet, dusky pink; Little Blue Baby, pale blue; Lilac Time, delicate lilac-mauve; and Niobe, pure white.

Chapter 6

THE VALUABLE GERANIUMS

Its ability to withstand drought — The attractive use of bloom and foliage — Cultural requirements — Planting in the boxes — Zonal Pelargoniums — Variegated-leaf geraniums — Dwarf geraniums — Ivy-leaf geraniums — Scented-leaf geraniums.

Due to the rich colouring of their bloom and foliage, great freedom of flowering, and ability to withstand long periods of drought, the geranium or pelargonium is by far the most important plant for window box culture. So great is the range of this family that books have been devoted entirely to it, a plant so beloved by Victorians and now happily returning to favour.

The geranium is one of the easiest of plants to manage. It is completely happy growing under town conditions and though it will thrive in a position of full sun, the plants will also flourish in partial shade. For full sun, the bedding and ivy-leaf geraniums should be planted; in partial shade, the ornamental and scented-leaf varieties, which are grown almost entirely for their interesting foliage. The plants remain tolerant of adverse weather, yet will stand up to long periods without moisture. For this reason they are valuable where the window box has to be left unattended during summer for long periods, often as long as two or three weeks at a time. A native of South Africa, the geranium is at its best under hot conditions and no plant withstands the blazing sunshine better. For which reason the plants are most suitable for use in the drier and more sunny parts of Britain, such as East Anglia and along the South Coast. They should always be used in preference to most other summer flowering plants for hotel and office window boxes and where they cannot be given quite as much attention as they should.

And yet the geranium family has still to regain that enormous popularity it enjoyed during the nineteenth century; the ornamental and scented-leaf varieties in particular still remaining sadly neglected. These colourful and interesting plants have also an additional value in that after the summer and autumn window box display, the plants may be taken indoors to be placed in a frost-free room where, kept almost dry at the roots, they will continue to provide colour through the winter. Here they retain their leaves and are almost perpetually flowering. Or the plants may be wintered in a warm greenhouse, where cuttings may be taken and rooted, the stock plants being used again and again for window box display.

Again, the plants will be less troubled by pest and disease than almost any other plant. Apart from their dislike of frost, they are almost foolproof. Nowhere are geraniums seen to better advantage than planted in the window boxes around the first court of Peterhouse, Cambridge. There, massed in each of the many dozens of boxes, the pink ivy-leaf Madame

Crousse is used to the exclusion of all others, beautifying those same buildings which were erected in 1286 and which were the beginning of the collegiate system in Europe. This lovely old college is well worthy of a visit for its window boxes alone.

All members of this large family should be planted out towards the end of May in the more favourable districts; the first week in June elsewhere. They are best grown on in 3½in. pots and transferred to bottomless whalehide pots of similar size when they are to be planted in the boxes. They may also be planted directly into the boxes after careful removal from the pots. Those who have a small greenhouse, glass porch, or sun-room, and where there is sufficient heat to exclude frost, may grow the plants entirely without pots and when lifting in late autumn, the plants may be placed in boxes of soil, to winter. Both foliage and roots should be kept as free from moisture as possible, otherwise the stems will tend to damp off near the base.

Greatly in the geranium's favour is its long flowering season, for when growing indoors the plants will generally be full of buds when planted in the window boxes early in summer. They will therefore come almost immediately into bloom and remain colourful until the end of October when the plants should be removed for fear of frost and also to make way for the

THE ATTRACTIVE USE OF
BLOOM AND FOLIAGE

The scarlet and pink zonal geraniums, so called because of the zone on their large round leaves, are at their best against a stone wall, or a wall washed with Snowcem which brings out their colouring to the full. For a cottage window box, the less formal ivy-leaf varieties with their semi-trailing habit and great freedom of flowering are delightful, and are also most suitable for tubs and garden vases. The ivy-leaf variety Eastbourne Beauty, with its velvety blood-red blooms and the pure white zonal,

Venus, is a most striking colour combination. Also the two ivy-leaf varieties together, the salmon-pink Ryecroft Surprise with the powder-mauve Mrs. Perrin, will provide a most charming combination.

Mrs. W. A. R. Clifton, with its double bloom of vivid flame, is attractive planted with the wonderful variegated-leaf variety, Mountains of Snow, its rich green leaves being edged with white. Also plant the ivy-leaf Orchard Blossom from America, with its flesh-pink blooms, with the variegated Happy Thought, of similar habit, its bright green leaves having an attractive golden butterfly at the centre. Several of the ornamental-leaf varieties may be planted together. Use Salmon Black Vesuvius with its bronze-black foliage or Golden Harry Hieover. Both grow only 4in. tall and are suitable for the front of the box. Back them with Mrs. Henry Cox or Marechal McMahon with their tricoloured leaves of gold, bronze, red and cream.

A single early tulip, Prince Carnival, suit-able for window box growing

Some Dutch crocus which give such a splash of colour to the spring window box

The variegated-leaf varieties planted with the bedding or zonal geraniums are lovely, using Mountains of Snow or the silver-leaved Lass O' Gowrie, with the huge double crimson-flowered Edmund Lachenal. Or plant the double white Hermine which is extremely free flowering with the orange scarlet Gustave Emich. The double oyster-pink Mrs. Lawrence planted with the cerise and white Monsieur Emil David is also a pleasing combination. The use of the ornamentals brighten up the window box when possibly there is little bloom from the other varieties during a sunless period; or they may be planted with the scented-leaf varieties in the more sunless positions.

The scented-leaf varieties do not bear particularly colourful flowers, but are amongst the most attractive of all plants, not only for their distinctive fragrance but for the appearance of their leaves. *P. asperium,* for instance, has laciniated fern-like foliage which, when pressed, emits a powerful lemon fragrance. The variety Prince of Orange makes a neat bushy plant of feathery habit, its small bright green leaves having a powerful orange perfume. There is the Pheasant's Foot geranium; one with oak-leaf foliage, another with gooseberry-like foliage. Each emit different scents and they may be planted together or used with other sections of this interesting family such as the Irene strain, full blossomed and compact.

CULTURAL REQUIREMENTS

The plants are quite happy in any ordinary loamy soil enriched with a small quantity of decayed cow or farmyard manure, and the soil must not lack lime. Geraniums, in other words, will grow well in any well-prepared window box soil to which has been incorporated some grit or coarse sand. When growing on the plants from cuttings, which may be taken at almost any time of the year, one may provide exactly the right conditions in which the plants may be grown.

The plants are kept in shape by

removing any long shoots and these may be rooted and grown on as replacement stock. The cutting should be removed immediately below a leaf joint and should be from 3in. to 4in. in length. Carefully remove all but the top two leaves and place the cutting in a sunny window or on a greenhouse bench for two to three hours before planting. This will allow some of the moisture to dry out and this will encourage quicker rooting. Cuttings may be taken and rooted at any time except during December and January when they may damp off before rooting. In any case, during the winter months give no moisture at all. Through all stages, geraniums demand dry soil conditions and the minimum of watering.

To root the cuttings, insert them round the sides of pots in a soil containing 50 per cent coarse sand and grit. In such a compost they will root in three weeks. As soon as well rooted, and they will root in any sunny window, the young plants should be re-potted into small 3in. pots composed of soil containing sand or grit and some decayed manure. Do not plant too deeply and water as little as possible. After several weeks the plants will have filled the pots with roots, when they should be re-potted into 3½in. pots containing similar compost. Their growing point should then be removed to encourage the formation of basal shoots, so as to build up a shapely, compact plant. Cuttings taken and rooted in early June will make sizeable plants for use in the window boxes the following June.

The plants will continue to grow throughout the summer and so must be given plenty of room. Geraniums do not like too close planting, for if a wet summer is experienced the foliage may be troubled by mildew. Allow them room to expand and to receive a free circulation of air. As an alternative to using dwarf geraniums for an edging, use the trailing lobelia Sapphire, its bright blue colouring being particularly attractive with pink flowering geraniums. It must, however, be said that geraniums, with the possible exception of lobelia and the attractive blue and white ageratums, always appear happiest when planted by themselves, and indeed, with their ability to withstand drier conditions than most other plants, they should almost always be planted without the company of other plants.

PLANTING IN THE BOXES

When preparing the window box, use fresh pasture loam, or if using town soil incorporate some lime rubble or give a good dressing with lime. Though geraniums will grow well under town conditions, this does not mean they will flourish in the generally acid soil of a town garden. The ideal is a pasture loam, to which is incorporated some grit and thoroughly decayed manure, preferably cow manure. The compost must be friable and well drained, and give 4oz. of bone meal to the average sized window box.

Do not set out the plants too early or they may be blackened by late frosts.

Keep them growing on, either in a cool greenhouse or room and where growing in the home always select as light a position as possible for the zonal varieties. Those grown for their foliage will grow well in partial shade.

Throughout summer remove the dead flower heads and any leaves which appear shrivelled, as soon as they form. To allow them to remain on the plants will not only give the boxes an untidy appearance, but will prevent the formation of new bloom. An occasional watering with dilute liquid manure will also help to prolong the flowering season and will ensure larger and more brilliantly coloured bloom. Those plants growing in town window boxes will receive great benefit from an occasional syringing with clean water during a dry period. This will both freshen the plants and remove soot deposits from the foliage, thus enabling them to retain their attractive bright green and variegated colourings.

Plants which are to be confined to

their pots throughout summer should be placed on a bed of soil in the window box, and a mixture of peat and soil should be packed round the pots to prevent undue moisture evaporation from the compost in the pots. As with all plants grown on in pots, see that the rim of the pot does not show above the sides of the window box. If required, trailing lobelia may be planted in the soil pockets between the pots.

It should be said that the taller growing Show or Regal pelargoniums, with their larger and more flimsy flowers are not suitable for window box culture unless in a particularly sheltered but sunny position. Even so, their habit is against their popularity for outdoor culture.

BEDDING GERANIUMS OR ZONAL PELARGONIUMS

The following varieties are highly suitable for window boxes.

AUDREY. The refined blooms are semi-double and of a pleasing shade of Rose Bengal.

BANBURY CROSS. A striking variety, the single blooms having a sparkling white eye.

BETTY CATCHPOLE. A new variety bearing single bright salmon-pink blooms.

CALEDONIA. The huge single blooms are of quite a new shade of satin-lilac.

COLONEL DRABBE. One of the most striking of all geraniums, the fully double deep crimson blooms have a white rayed centre.

DECORATOR. The semi-double blooms are of a distinct shade of cherry-red.

EDMUND LACHENAL. A beauty. The large double blooms being of a rich velvety crimson colour.

EDWARD HUMPHRIS. Makes a bushy plant and is very free flowering, bearing masses of single flowers of pure white.

E. HERBERT. A lovely variety, the double blooms being of shell-pink over a white ground.

GUSTAVE EMICH. Of compact habit, its double blooms of intense orange-scarlet are freely produced.

HUGO DE VRIES. A new introduction, the huge truss of double blooms being of a deep shade of peach-pink.

JOHN CROSS. The single bloom is of an attractive shade of salmon-pink with a distinct silvery sheen.

LAVE. The bloom is not large, but very double and of a vivid shade of purest orange.

LE COLOSSE. A new variety bearing huge double blooms of a unique shade of brick red.

LORD CURZON. The large single purple bloom has a pronounced white eye.

MADAME RECOMIER. Excellent for a window box, the plant is of compact habit, the white flowers being fully double.

PAUL CRAMPEL. The excellent and well known vivid scarlet.

PAUL REBOUX. A superb variety, the double bloom being of richest crimson-red.

RED RAMBLER. This is quite a distinct variety, bearing tiny round double blooms, like a red rambler rose.

SALMONIA. This is a fine variety for a window box. The leaves are small and darkest green, whilst masses of small, butterfly-like flowers of a lovely salmon-orange colour are borne on long graceful stems.

SANSOVINO. The single blooms are large and of a glowing orange-salmon shade.

SUSAN BALDWIN. The single blooms are of a lovely shade of purest salmon-pink.

THE SPEAKER. Fine for a window box, the blooms being of a delicate shade of salmon-pink.

THOMAS EARLE. A fine variety, the large single blooms being of a striking blood-red colour.

WILLINGDON GEM. A most striking variety, the single blooms being large and of a delicate shade of orange-pink with a large white centre.

VARIEGATED-LEAF GERANIUMS

A HAPPY THOUGHT. Most striking, the dark green leaf having a golden 'butterfly' marking in the centre. It bears masses of small but dainty brick-red blooms.

CAROLINE SCHMIDT. Its bright silver leaves and double scarlet flowers make this an excellent variety.

CRYSTAL PALACE GEM. A fine short-jointed plant, the golden-yellow leaves being attractively marked with green 'butterflies'.

MARECHAL MCMAHON. The golden leaf has zones of green and bronze. The compact habit is ideal for window box culture.

MISS FARREN. Outstanding, with its attractive large green and silver zoned leaves.

MRS. POLLOCK. The large flat leaves are beautifully zoned yellow, green and bronzy-purple.

TURTLE'S SURPRISE. An ancient variety happily re-discovered. Of compact habit, its double crimson bloom is equal to that of the best bedding geraniums, whilst they are held on long pure white stems. The foliage has a pretty 'butterfly' centre. Altogether a most outstanding variety.

BERONA. Lovely for planting with scarlet zonal varieties, for its bright golden-green leaves are quite zone-less and make a pleasing contrast.

DWARF GERANIUMS

These miniature geraniums, with their richly coloured leaves, are delightful plants for the front of a window box, or for the main display for a small box.

BLACK VESUVIUS. Very slow growing, a fully grown plant will reach a height of 4in. to 5in. bearing scarlet flowers and bronzy-black foliage. Striking when used with Madame Salleroi. There is another form bearing deep salmon flowers.

DISTINCTION. Most colourful, bearing vivid green leaves with a jet black ring round the edge and crimson flowers.

GOLDEN HARRY HIEOVER. Bearing a glossy golden leaf with a crimson zone and numerous vermilion flowers, this is a most striking variety.

LASS O' GOWRIE. One of the most

colourful of all dwarf geraniums. The silver leaves are marked green, gold and red, whilst the plant bears a small, but brilliant single red flower.

LITTLE TROT. Has small, silvery white leaves and dainty pink flowers.

MADAME SALLEROI. It does not bloom, but the tiny bush-like plants, with their brilliant silver leaves, are quite enchanting.

MEPHISTOPHELES. Almost a replica of Black Vesuvius, but grows about 2in. taller, whilst the foliage is even darker.

IVY-LEAF GERANIUMS

ABEL CARRIERE. A fine variety bearing huge double Tyrian purple blooms.

BEAUTY OF CASTLEHILL. A vigorous bloomer, bearing double deep rose-coloured flowers.

EULALIA. Possibly the old Blue Ivy-leaf, bearing very double deep blue-mauve flowers amidst deep green foliage.

KING EDWARD VII. This variety is not nearly so widely grown as it should be, the very large blooms being of a rich shade of rose-cerise.

MADAME CROUSSE. The popular free-flowering pink.

MRS. W. A. R. CLIFTON. Its bright green leaves and very double blooms of rich blood-red make this a fine window box variety.

RYECROFT SURPRISE. Of upright habit, the refined blooms are of a beautiful shade of salmon-pink.

SIR PERCY BLAKENEY. An excellent variety, the large double blooms being of a deep crimson colour.

SCENTED-LEAF GERANIUMS

Most attractive with their interesting leaf variations and scents, not all are suitable for window box culture. *P. tomentosum,* with its hairy stems and flat woolly leaves, and the tall growing *P. crispum major,* though making charming indoor pot plants are not suitable for a window box or for outdoor planting. There are, however, many that are suitable.

ENDSLEIGH. Its broad, dark green leaf smells of pepper, but it is of handsome appearance.

FAIR HELEN. Of dwarf, compact habit, the dark oak-leaved foliage possesses a strong smell of incense.

P. ASPERIUM. Its deeply serrated leaves and oily pungent smell make it most attractive for planting with the brilliantly-flowered zonals.

P. DENTICULATUM. The fern-like appearance of the foliage, with its refreshing lemon fragrance, make it deal for window box planting.

P. FILICIFOLIUM. Its glossy serrated leaves emit an oily pungence and are quite sticky to the touch.

PRETTY POLLY. Dwarf and bushy and with a strong scent of almonds.

PRINCE OF ORANGE. A really lovely variety for 'mixing' with the more colourful varieties. The foliage is of a vivid green colour, produced in fairy-like abundance and smelling strongly of oranges.

P. STENOPETALUM. The rich green leaves are of ivy shape and smell strongly of wormwood.

ROYAL OAK. A striking variety,

with large dark green oak-leaf foliage, which makes a pleasing contrast with the brighter coloured variegated-leaf varieties.

Chapter 7
THE MINIATURE ROSES

Their value for window box and trough garden — Their culture — Varieties.

In this age of restricted gardening, the miniature roses are ideal plants, requiring very little attention and remaining long in bloom. They are quite inexpensive and may be used in so many ways, and especially are they delightful used in stone troughs or in a sunny window box where they remain in bloom from early summer until well into autumn.

The plants are perfectly hardy, withstanding the severest of weather, but they are more readily established if pot grown, when they may be planted at any time except when the soil is frozen. Pot grown plants are well worth the extra cost, for if correctly tended they will prove very long lasting. They should not, however, be planted in the window box in their pots, for in this way they may suffer from lack of moisture during a dry period.

THEIR CULTURE

They are happiest in a well-drained loam. Marl containing some coarse sand is ideal but do not give any manure or the plants will produce excessive foliage at the expense of bloom. They will, however, benefit from 2oz. of bone meal per square foot worked into the soil just before planting. Throughout the summer months the plants will respond to an application of weak manure water once each week.

As it is important that the plants do not suffer from lack of moisture, it is advisable when growing in troughs or window boxes to incorporate some peat or leaf mould to help retain moisture, and always make quite certain that there is ample drainage. Firm planting is essential and allow the plants room to develop. They are quite small when set out but soon grow into dense little bushes, though rarely exceeding 8in. to 9in. in height. When planting in troughs, place the ball of earth just below the level of the soil, for shoots which appear from below the ground will also bear bloom. These should be cut back half way at the end of each season, likewise any unduly vigorous shoots and decayed wood. And remember to remove all dead blooms as they form, otherwise flowering will quickly end.

Where growing in window boxes, it will be advisable to knock the plants from their pots and re-plant into bottomless whalehide pots which will enable the roots to search for moisture and food. The top of the pot should be placed almost at soil level and when the plants are lifted in late autumn to make way for winter and spring flowering plants, the soil ball will be almost intact. These plants may then be replanted into earthenware pots which are plunged into the open ground to winter. Where the plants are to remain permanently in the window box or trough, they may be planted directly into the soil.

A delightful display may be enjoyed by planting with them several of the miniature conifers and arranging both the roses and conifers in small groups. So that there may be colour during winter and spring, pots of small flowering bulbs, such as the chionodoxas and scillas may be planted. In this way the roses may remain undisturbed for several years and there will thus be almost all-year-round colour, with the very minimum of trouble and expense.

The fairy roses are delightful plants for growing in a sunny window indoors in 60 size pots, but it is advisable to winter them in the open ground and to remove indoors in early June when coming into bud. They seem to lose vitality if kept continuously indoors.

VARIETIES

One of the loveliest varieties is Josephine Wheatcroft, which bears bloom the size of a five-penny piece, of a rich shade of yellow, the bloom being tapered in the true hybrid tea form. For a buttonhole or for table decoration, the cut bloom is charming.

The other varieties bear a bloom more like a polyantha rose and outstanding is Baby Masquerade, the pale yellow blooms being splashed with red, whilst equally lovely are the large deep-pink blooms of Tinker Bell. Most attractive when planted together are Maid Marion, with its double crimson button-like blooms, and the double white, edged pink Cinderella, Equally free flowering is Humpty Dumpty, glistening pink; and Sweet Dumpty, glistening pink; and Sweet Fairy, the blooms being of a pleasing shade of mauve-pink and very full. Both varieties are very dwarf.

Striking is Perle d'Alcanada, with its blooms of deep carmine-red, beautifully formed like a tea rose; whilst the creamy-white Pour Toi, growing to a height of 10in., is ideal for a window box. Excellent, too, is the shell-pink Simple Simon. Two varieties, Granada, blood red, and Red Imp, bright carmine, are most showy in either the bush or standard form. In the bush form, the plants reach a height of 9in. and about 16in. as miniature standards.

A lovely introduction, making a plant about 9in. tall is Presumida, bearing circular fully double blooms of rich apricot, edged with gold. Baby Gold Star, of similar height, and with its blooms of a deep buttercup yellow, is also lovely; also the true guinea gold, Rosina. Of those of taller habit, another suitable variety for a window box is Perle de Montserrat, its blooms being of a peach-pink colour. Each of these taller growing varieties are ideal for a window box, those of more dwarf habit being more suitable for sinks and trough gardens. Of these, in addition to Sweet Fairy, Mon. Petit, with its very full blooms of a deep rose-pink colour; Pixie, purest white; and Twinkles, palest shell-pink, are quite charming.

For a larger window box, the Walt Disney Compacta roses, really miniature floribundas, are most colourful and must have a great future. They grow to a height of from 12in. to 14in., the bloom being borne in compact trusses. The plants require exactly the same treatment as described for the miniature roses and very little pruning.

The plants are extremely tolerant of adverse weather and remain free from pest and disease, their glossy green foliage taking on a most healthy appearance.

Possibly the outstanding variety is Grumpy, its crimson-red blooms having an attractive white centre. Also with a white centre are the scarlet single blooms of Bashful. An attractive variety bearing fully double blooms of deep pink, is Sleepy, whilst Doc bears a bloom of salmon-pink, held in large trusses. The whole range of these dwarf roses is most delightful and ideal in every way for summer and autumn window box display.

Chapter 8
ANNUALS FOR THE WINDOW BOX

Annuals in the cropping programme — Raising the plants — Making up the boxes — Ageratum — Alonsoa —

Antirrhinum — Aster — Balsam — Brachycome — Cornflower — Eschscholtzia — Godetia — Lobelia — Marigold — Matthiola — Mesembryan- themum — Mignonette — Nasturtium — Nemesia — Pansy — Petunia — Phlox Drummondii — Tagetes — Ver- bena — Virginia Stock.

The use of annuals in the window box will depend much upon its use for the spring display. Where late spring and early summer flowering plants are being used, such as double tulips, winter-flowering violas and the numerous miniature bulbs, then the boxes cannot be made up until early in June. This will mean that the annuals, whether hardy or half-hardy, must be either purchased from a nursery at the time the boxes are to be made up, or the plants must have been grown on in small pots or boxes from an early spring or autumn sowing. In which case either a cold frame or cloches will be necessary. However, it would seem that as a general rule the half-hardy annuals, e.g. dwarf African and French marigolds and the petunias should follow late spring flowering plants. They will have been raised in a warm greenhouse sowing the seed in the New Year, the plants being thoroughly hardened before planting in the boxes. In any case, the less hardy plants should not be planted out before the beginning of June.

Hardy annuals will either be sown directly into the boxes, though except for one or two varieties this is rarely successful, or they will have been sown in early autumn and wintered under a frame or under cloches. The plants which will respond to this almost biennial treatment are the dwarf antirrhinums and pansies, both of which are really perennial but are almost always given hardy annual treatment. The cornflower, too, may be sown in autumn. Those hardy annuals which may, and on account of their resentment of root disturbance should, be sown directly into the window box where they are to bloom, are the eschscholtzia, godetia and Virginia stock. The nasturtium is almost always sown where it is to bloom though it will readily transplant.

These plants may therefore be used where the boxes are free before the end of April, or where an inner or replacement box is used. Most of these hardy annuals may be expected to come into bloom quite quickly from seed sown directly in the replacement box. If sown in the fixed box there will be a period of at least eight weeks when there will be no colour, though this may be partly overcome by replanting several of the winter violas which remain perpetually in bloom.

Only those plants should be used for a window box which are of compact, free flowering habit, and which will remain in bloom until well into the autumn. The plants are then replaced by those which will continue the display into winter and spring. For edging the box, the ageratum and sweet alyssum remain in bloom longer than the lobelias, the ageratum being outstanding on account of its more upright habit. The mesembryanthemum, the Waldersee aster, the petunia, and all members of the marigold family are also long flowering, the blooms continuing to appear until November. Each of these plants, too, are well able to withstand a sun-baked position and periods of drought which make them additionally suited to window box culture. Where annuals are to be used one or more of these plants should be given first choice. Where the box is given a partially shaded aspect facing due north or east, the dwarf nasturtiums and pansies and violas should be used. Of those plants which are to be sown directly into the box during April or early May, the godetias edged with the tiny eschscholtzia and miniature primrose will provide a colourful display and remain long in bloom.

RAISING THE PLANTS

Plants of the half-hardy annuals will either be obtained from a nursery or will be raised in a warm greenhouse. Where neither method is practicable, then it will be necessary to use those plants given hardy or biennial treatment and wintered under a frame or cloches, or the plants may be raised from a March sowing under cloches or frames. In either case, the seed should be sown in boxes containing one of the soil-less composts or the John Innes Sowing Compost made up as follows:—

2 parts loam preferably sterilised ....)
1 part coarse sand ....)
1 part peat ....) per
1½ oz. superphosphate) bushel
of lime ....)
¾ oz. ground limestone ....)

Sow the seed thinly, water after sowing and unless conditions are dry give no more moisture until the seed has germinated. If sown in a frame, the seed should be put in early in September or early in March. Half-hardy annuals should be sown in January in gentle heat. As soon as large enough to handle, the seedlings should be pricked out into boxes containing a similar compost, to which should be added 2oz. of bone meal and 1oz. of sulphate of potash per bushel. An excellent method is to make small soil blocks of this compost. These are placed in boxes and into each block a seedling is planted. There will thus be no disturbance of the roots when planted in the window boxes. Again, should the display of spring plants be later than expected, there will be no undue hurry to plant out the annuals, as there may be if the plants have been grown in boxes and growth has been rapid. Alternatively, the plants may be grown on in 2½in. pots. The more expensive seed, such as that of the petunia and antirrhinum, which is extremely small, should be sown on the top of the compost and only lightly covered with sand. A sheet of glass should be placed over the box, and over this should be placed a sheet of brown paper to be removed immediately the seed has germinated.

Plants which have been grown under cold conditions will require very little hardening, but the half-hardy annuals raised in heat must be gradually accustomed to outdoor conditions before planting in the boxes. Should there be no cold frame, plants raised in heat should be grown cold for several weeks, and from the beginning of May should be placed outdoors in a sheltered position on all favourable days, at first being taken indoors in the evening then being allowed to remain outside entirely unprotected by day and by night.

The value of raising one's own plants is that one may grow the variety of one's choice, whilst one may know that the plants are grown well and are thoroughly hardened. The range of annuals for window box culture has greatly widened during the post war decade, the hybridizers realizing the trend towards small gardens and gardening in restricted places.

MAKING UP THE BOXES

The compost of the window box for annual plants should consist of a fibrous loam, preferably removed from old pasture, for it will then be almost devoid of weed seeds and be sweet and fresh. Soil taken from a town garden should not be used, for it will generally be of an acid nature owing to constant deposits of soot and sulphur, whilst it may contain weed seeds and be troubled by pest and disease. Where possible, obtain soil removed from a pasture or soil taken from a country garden which has been sterilized. To the soil should be added a small quantity of coarse sand and two or three handfuls of horticultural peat to keep it 'open' and help to retain moisture. Add 2oz. of bone meal to the average size box, a sprinkling of lime and a few pieces of charcoal to keep it sweet. The compost will then be ready for the plants. When filling the box, allow ½in. from the top of the soil to the top of the box, otherwise when watering, or during a period of heavy rain, the soil will be splashed over the side, causing unsightliness both to the box, which may have been newly painted, and to the walls of the house.

When planting, make quite certain

that the compost has settled down, and do not overcrowd the boxes. Plant firmly and, as with planting out in beds, select as dull and moist a period as possible. Allow the plants room to develop by not planting too closely. For antirrhinums, asters, petunias, cornflowers and the mesembry-anthemums, plant 4in. apart. Pansies, nemesia, marigolds and the ageratum may be planted 3in. apart. And do not attempt to use too great a variety. A striking combination is orange anti-rrhinums with yellow marigolds, or the petunias in various colours look most striking planted together. The same remarks appertain to window box planting as with planting in the open ground, the time will depend upon the situation and upon the hardiness of the plants to be used. Some protection from cold winds may be given by pres-sing pieces of plywood down the sides of the box until the plants have become established.

When growing from seed, it may be necessary in a built-up area to give protection from birds by placing black thread 2in. above soil level until the young plants have become established. Thinning of those plants which make bushy growth will be necessary and this should not be too long delayed. Those annuals which do not like root disturbance should be sown directly into boxes, or planting may be done from pots or soil blocks which are proving most useful in raising those plants which do not enjoy transplanting.

The plants should be kept comfortably moist and when once they come into bloom, occasional waterings with dilute liquid manure will help to prolong the display. Liquid manure in concentrated form may be obtained from most seed stores in small bottles and is free from any unpleasant smell.

To prevent splashing which may be caused by heavy rain, the soil should be covered with fresh moss until the plants have made sufficient growth to cover the soil themselves. The moss will help to maintain moisture in the soil whilst the plants are becoming established.

SUITABLE WINDOW BOX ANNUALS
((H.H.) = Half-hardy)

AGERATUM (H.H.). There are a number of new and most valuable varieties of this excellent window box plant, each of them being of compact habit and growing to a height of about 6in. Little Blue Star, with its fluffy navy-blue flowers; Capri, mid-blue; and Blue Mink, are all excellent. The new Blue Blazer and Blue Mink varieties cover themselves with flowers and are compact.

ALONSOA (H.H.). This is best raised by sowing two or three seeds to a 2½in. pot, for it does not take too kindly to root disturbance. When 3in. tall, the growing points should be pinched out to make compact plants. The best variety is *A. Warscewiczii compacta,* which bears its scarlet spikes like miniature sidalceas on 12in. to 14in. stems.

ANTIRRHINUM. Both the *nanum compactum* varieties which attain a height of 9in. to 10in. and the Tom Thumb varieties, which form compact carpets 8in. high and bloom in profusion, are ideal for window box culture. Autumn sown plants may be set out in early April and will come into bloom about June 1st, continuing until the end of October. Of the Tom Thumb varieties, Pinkie is outstanding, the small spikes being of a delicious combination of strawberry-pink and cream. This should be planted entirely on its own or with one of the ageratums. Or plant together Yellow Prince and Crimson King for a striking display.

Of the *nanum compactum* varieties Orange Queen, glowing orange with a pink throat; Coral Queen, soft pink with a white throat; and Scarlet and White Queen, the latter two planted together, make a most colourful display.

ASTER (H.H.). It is the dwarf Waldersee aster, making a bushy plant 9in. tall that is most valuable for a window box, though it comes rather late into bloom. If grown in small pots in the boxes, the plants may be taken indoors when the box is cleared in October and will continue to bloom until Christmas.

BALSAM (H.H.). This is one of the most tender of the annuals and should generally be used in the more favourable districts. The bush double-flowered strain, growing to a height of 12in. and bearing camellia-like blooms in pastel shades amidst glossy foliage is outstanding. The plants require careful hardening and should not be planted out until mid-June. They are best grown and planted in 60 size pots.

BRACHYCOME (H.H.). This, the Swan River daisy, is quite hardy though a native of Australia. It prefers a dry, sandy soil and a sunny position, where it bears its small starry purple flowers throughout summer and autumn. An attractive variety is Azure Fairy, the lavender flowers having a white zone.

CORNFLOWER. *Centaurea cyanus* is its correct name and though for long popular for cutting, the dwarf forms are ideal for window boxes, making bushy plants and growing to a height of only 10in.

The first of the dwarfs was Jubilee Gem with its rich cornflower blue flowers; then followed the lovely Lilac Lady and now, Rose Gem, all of which look most charming planted together.

ESCHSCHOLTZIA. Sow a few seeds where the plants are to bloom, of the variety Miniature Primrose, growing no taller than 5in. It is very tolerant of dry conditions.

GODETIA. This plant is best sown where it is to bloom or in small pots, for it resents root disturbance. One of the most compact varieties is Sybil Sherwood, the salmon-pink bloom being flushed with orange, and it rarely exceeds 12in. in height. But where a dwarf compact plant is required, Sutton's Dwarf Lavender, forming bushy little plants only 9in. tall and bearing masses of small lavender cups with attractive white centres, is excellent. Plant with it Crimson Glow, of similar habit, and edge the window box with Miniature Primrose eschscholtzia for a charming display.

LOBELIA. Though, like the anti-rrhinum, strictly a perennial, the lobelia is always given annual treatment, the seed being sown in heat in February, covering the seed only lightly with sand and covering the box or pan with a sheet of clean glass to hasten germination. Whilst being hardened, it is advisable to pinch back those shoots which tend to become straggly to encourage a bushy plant. The plants should be set out at the end of May or early in June when the spring bedding display has finished, the plants being used entirely for edging and should be spaced 5in. to 6in. apart.

Though the navy-blue, Mrs. Clibran, with its striking white eye, is the most widely planted of all lobelias, the paler Blue Stone is far more attractive planted with pink flowering plants, whilst the dark sea-blue Crystal Palace; the white Snowball; and the uncommon crimson-red Prima Donna, are all worth using by way of original-ity. Three or four varieties may be planted alternately to produce a colourful effect. The trailing variety, Sapphire, is excellent for covering the front of a window box, used especially with the more exotic annuals.

MARIGOLD (H.H.). It is not the calendula or pot marigold which is of value in a window box, but the tagetes forms, the dwarf French and African marigolds which rarely exceed 6in. in height. They are delightful plants for using towards the front of a box, or they may be planted entirely on their own, using one or two plants of each of the very wide variety of colours. These marigolds are extremely long flowering and are of sturdy, upright habit, and quite untroubled by adverse weather.

Though most of the African varieties are tall growing, the new Paprika, which bears large flame red flowers amidst fern-like foliage, grows only 6in. tall and makes a bushy plant. The French marigolds may now be obtained with the most arresting markings of mahogany and gold, the mark-

Polyanthus in glowing colours

One of the newer Ageratum—Sky Chief

Fiesta Multi Flora Double Begonias

A pleasant display of annuals

ings being quite unique amongst flowers. In the double-flowered section, the varieties Nugget, Brocade, Seven Star and many others provide the widest of choices. In the single-flowered, Naughty Marietta, a tiny compact plant, the golden blooms blotched and striped maroon are most unusual.

MATTHIOLA (H.H.). The fragrant stocks have long been valuable for window box culture, brought on in 60 size pots, in which they are best grown in the window box. The introduction of Hansens 100 per cent Double Strain, making compact plants only 9in. tall and producing their fragrant bloom over a long period, will give this plant even greater popularity. Seed may now be obtained in separate colours of the usual pastel shades, and the feature of this strain is that single plants may be detected in the seedling stage and destroyed. When the seedlings are ready for transplanting, having been raised in gentle heat, if the boxes are placed in a temperature of just under 45° F. for 48 hours it will be found that a small number of seedlings will have turned a dark green colour. These should be removed and destroyed, for they would produce only single blooms. The others are returned to the greenhouse, transplanted and grown on in a temperature of about 50° F. and the result will be 100 per cent doubles.

The plants should not be set out until towards the end of May, being planted 8in. apart in the beds. At all times keep the young plants as dry as possible, for they suffer from black-leg disease at any age. To ensure immunity it is necessary to use a sterilized soil. Water only when absolutely essential and then with Cheshunt Compound. The plants should be given fresh soil when potted. Apart from this give the usual half-hardy treatment.

MESEMBRYANTHEMUM (H.H.). These dwarf growing succulent plants, native of South Africa, should be given a sunny position and a dry, sandy soil. They will survive almost desert-like conditions, remaining in bloom throughout summer and autumn, the daisy-shaped flowers opening only when the sun shines on them. *M. criniflorum* is also known as the Livingstone daisy, and no annual has a more brilliant colour range with its blooms of crimson, pink, apricot and yellow and numerous art shades.

MIGNONETTE. It likes a soil containing some lime; also some humus. Though sweetly scented, the mignonette, *Reseda odorata,* has never, until recently, been conspicuous for the quality of its flowers. With the introduction of the large-flowered varieties, this plant has now become attractive, in addition to being so fragrant. The lovely deep yellow, Golden Goliath; the richly-coloured Crimson Giant; and the bright, Red Monarch, growing to a height of 12in. and making large branching plants, are a great improvement on the old mignonette.

NASTURTIUM. The dwarf double varieties Fireball, Jewel mixed, Golden Ball, and the cream-flushed pink

Aurora, together with the compact single, Ryburgh Perfection, make a colourful display in a window box. The seed is sown either directly into the box in April or in small pots to plant in the boxes as soon as clear of the spring flowering plants.

NEMESIA (H.H.). Like the marigolds, the modern nemesia has been improved out of all recognition during recent years, the habit being more compact, more free flowering and remaining longer in bloom. Though classed as being half-hardy they are almost hardy, and like the marigolds are ideal for a northern garden.

Both Blue Gem and Dwarf Orange, growing only 8in. tall, may be used for a window box. Also suitable are Harrison's Dwarf Compact Hybrids, which grow to a similar height. Aurora, carmine with white tip; Fire King, crimson-scarlet; and Orange Prince are most distinct, the individual blooms being as large as a fivepenny piece.

PANSY. Though perennial, the pansies are generally treated as biennials for window box culture, though the winter flowering varieties may be left to provide all-year-round colour. Seed should be sown in July so that the plants will make plenty of growth before the winter and the best method of raising the plants is to sow in shallow drills lined with peat. The seedlings should be transplanted to open ground beds into a soil containing plenty of humus, or to cold frames. There they will remain until ready for planting in the window boxes between early April and June when the plants will be showing bud and bloom. To prolong the display, remove all dead bloom as it forms and never allow the plants to lack moisture. Pansies will be happier where shaded from the midday sun.

Of the very numerous large-flowering varieties, Englemann's Giant strain, with its huge blooms of the most brilliant colours blotched with black, has long retained its popularity.

Those who prefer self colours will find the deep blue Ullswater; the golden-yellow Coronation Gold; the crimson Alpenglow; and White Lady all most colourful for a window box.

PETUNIA (H.H.). This is one of the more tender bedding plants requiring to be raised in heat and being planted out in early June. With their ruffled trumpets of the most intense colouring, great freedom of flowering and compact habit, no plant will make a more exotic display nor remain so colourful.

For outdoor planting the more compact dwarf bedding strains should be used. Petunias nowadays come in a bewildering array of new varieties, many of Fl. breeding, and many bred for their wet and rust repelling qualities. But the window box gardener will not go far wrong planting such hybrid strains as Joy, Cascade, All Double Canadian Wonder, Formula Mixed and the named colours in the Fl. hybrid strains such as Red Cap, Snow Cap, Rose Perfection, Red Ensign and Blue

Lustre.

The seed should be sown with care in the New Year, sowing in a warm greenhouse and pricking out the seedlings into individual 2½in. pots. Established plants like plenty of moisture at the roots and frequent syringing will keep the foliage free of aphis.

PHLOX DRUMMONDII (H.H.). For boxes, Sutton's Beauty strain, obtainable in numerous shades of pink and mauve and making compact plants 6in. tall, are delightful. Keep comfortably moist.

TAGETES (H.H.). *T. signata,* Golden Gem, bearing its golden blooms at a height of 8in. through summer and autumn is ideal for window boxes. Another variety, Paprika, bears crimson-red flowers.

VERBENA (H.H.). This delightful bedding plant is yet another of those tender perennials which is always given half-hardy treatment. In the north there is a tendency for the plants to come rather too late into bloom, being at their best during late August and through September. In the south the plants, from a February sowing in heat, come into bloom at the end of July. Some of the best varieties for a window box are Blaze (scarlet), Sparkle Mixed and Compact. Unlike most verbenas they are of compact, upright habit, the shoots requiring no pegging down. The plants enjoy a position of full sun, but do like a moist soil.

VIRGINIA STOCK. To provide indoor fragrance, sow a double row to the front of a box early in April, making a second sowing at the back of the box mid-May to provide a succession of fragrant bloom.

Chapter 9
COLOURED FOLIAGE PLANTS

The value of foliage plants for the summer window box — Arabis variegata — Begonia Rex — Centaurea — Cerastium tomentosum — Cineraria maritima — Coleus — Eriophyllum integrifolium — Euryops Evansii — Geranium, Ornamental-leaf —

Leucophyta Brownei — Pyrethrum Parthenium.

Nowhere are coloured foliage plants used to better advantage than in the window box where they may be used as a contrast to the more richly flowering plants, or they may be planted by themselves. As with so many plants, those which bear coloured foliage are not always good mixers and whereas the ornamental geraniums, described in Chapter 6 are outstanding when used either by themselves or with other members of the same family, likewise Begonia Rex, they would look quite out of place planted with most annuals. Both these plants may be grown on in 5in. pots, the window box being used merely as a container to hold the pots, or they may be planted into bottomless whalehide pots and inserted in a box containing the correct compost. Again, they may be set out directly into the soil of the box just as they are when planted in beds. The other plants to be described here and which are generally treated as annuals will be planted directly into the box along with other summer-flowering annuals.

ARABIS VARIEGATA. With its compact habit and woolly leaves of silver and gold, the arabis is a most useful plant for spring and early summer bedding. It grows to a height of 6in. and remains compact for a long time. It should be planted with the other spring flowering plants and may be removed to make way for the summer display early in June. Propagation is by cuttings which will root quickly if inserted in a sandy soil during summer.

BEGONIA REX. In comparison with the ornamental geraniums, the ornamental-leaf begonias require considerably more attention for they are copious drinkers. For this reason they should be used only where they may receive the necessary attention and where boxes may easily be reached. They are best used in a box which is sheltered from the mid-day sun, for in this way the plants do not dry out so rapidly, neither does the sun bleach their attractively marked foliage. Like their geranium counterpart, the ornamental-leaf begonias are evergreen and after providing summer colour in the boxes, should be removed to a frost-proof position indoors early in October to continue the display.

Plants which are to be confined to their pots should have moist peat packed round the pots to prevent drying out of the roots during periods of drought. The peat should be kept moist together with the compost in the pots. The Rex begonias grow from a rhizome, or semi-tuber, which tends to grow horizontally rather than deep down into the pot, and so the plants will appreciate an occasional top dressing or mulch of leaf mould, or a peat and soil mixture, when they have become established. The usual John Innes potting compost suits them well, adding just a little more sand than suggested, whilst the peat may be substituted with leaf mould.

The best method of propagation is

by stem cuttings removed from the base of the plants where they are generally numerous, and the best time to take them is just before the plants are placed in the boxes early in June. One or two may be carefully removed from each plant without harming the shape. They should be rooted, like geranium cuttings, round the sides of a 48 size pot in a compost made up of loam, leaf mould and silver sand in equal quantities by bulk. They should not be over-watered. In a cool greenhouse, or sunny window, the cuttings will root in three weeks when they should be potted into 2½in. pots and again into 60 size pots towards the end of summer. By June of the following season they will have made plenty of foliage and will be just right for the boxes.

There are many striking named varieties of Begonia Rex. Lympstone is excellent, the silver-green leaf having dark green veins; whilst Rougemont bears a bright cherry-red leaf, edged with pink. Himalaya is also striking, the dark green leaves being splashed with silver, whilst the pink and mauve leaves of Welcome are attractively bordered with silver. An occasional application of dilute liquid manure will enhance the colourings.

CENTAUREA. Though better known members of this huge family are the cornflowers and sweet sultan, it is those bearing silvery foliage that are most useful for window boxes. *C. Argentea* **and** *C. Clementei,* **both of compact habit and bearing silvery-grey fern-like foliage, are of the same family as** *Cineraria maritima,* **and similar in every way. Propagation is from seed sown under glass in May, the plants being wintered under glass for planting out the following May; or short cuttings may be taken just before the plants are set out and rooted under glass, round the side of a pot. In exposed districts the plants will be happier wintered in gentle heat.**

CERASTIUM TOMENTOSUM. **This extremely hardy perennial is commonly known as Snow in Summer, for its covers itself in masses of pretty,** pure white cup-shaped blooms throughout summer and well into winter. It flowers continuously except during the mid-winter months. It is a plant of semi-trailing habit, bearing silvery-grey leaves, so that it may be planted along the edge of a window box where it may remain permanently. All straggling shoots must be cut back early in spring. Propagation may be either from seed sown in boxes in May, the seedlings being transplanted into small pots at the end of summer, or the plants may be increased by rooting cuttings under a frame or cloche during summer. For edging a window box or for planting in a trough garden, *C. alpinum lanatum,* making a little tufted plant only 2in. to 3in. tall, with its foliage a bright silvery-grey colour, is most pleasing.

CINERARIA MARITIMA. This is not quite such a good plant for window box culture as the leucophyta, as it grows rather taller, reaching a height of about 15in. The plants may, however, be kept more dwarf if the leading shoots are kept pinched back and this will also prevent them forming their inconspicuous yellow flowers, for the charm of the plant lies in its deeply cut leaves of silvery-grey which are covered with a silver down.

It may be propagated by sowing seed in a closed frame or in heat in May or June, for it does not germinate quickly and must be given a full twelve months in which to reach the stage in which it is required for bedding out. The seedlings are transplanted when large enough to handle, and again to 3in. pots, in which they remain over winter. The plants are set out at the end of May with many of the other summer bedding plants.

A more rapid method of increasing the stock is to remove the twiggy shoots in May. These are inserted round the sides of pots containing coarse sand and peat, where they will form roots in about four to five weeks. They are then moved to 3in. pots placed in open frames, where they are kept growing through summer. They may be wintered in closed frames or in a cold house, but in cold districts are happier in gentle heat. The plants will become more bushy and compact if pinched back occasionally.

Cineraria maritima is delightful used with the dwarf Waldersee asters, for its foliage does show off the deep pink and purple colours of the asters to best advantage. It is also pleasing used with pink or scarlet antirrhinums.

COLEUS. So well known for greenhouse culture, where its richly-coloured and variegated leaves are always admired, little is seen of the coleus in outdoor beds, though several species are suitable and are most attractive when planted with the other foliage plants and edged with feather-few. But in the same way as the coleus enjoys a moist, rather humid atmosphere when in the greenhouse, so it does outdoors, otherwise it will drop its petals as it does when in the warm, dry atmosphere of a room. It is therefore better used for bedding in the west, especially in the warm, moist climate of the south-west. The best species for outdoors is *C. Verschaffelti,* the cuttings of which are struck in early March in sand and, as soon as rooted, which they readily do, they should be potted into 3in. pots containing loam and rotted manure. After hardening they are planted out in early June and must be kept well watered, both foliage and roots.

ERIOPHYLLUM INTEGRIFOLIUM. This is a delightful plant for a window box which receives the full mid-day sunshine during summer. The plant has a dainty silvery-green leaf and covers itself with orange-yellow flowers from early June until September. It grows to a height of 10in. and is most useful to plant with the maritime cineraria and the leucophyta, making a display of rich silver. To accentuate the silver colour, plant just one or two scarlet geraniums or multiflora begonias for an original and striking summer display.

GERANIUM, ornamental-leaf. See Chapter 6.

LEUCOPHYTA BROWNEI. This interesting and colourful plant remains comparatively unknown, only on rare occasions is it to be found even in our parks and country house gardens, used as a contrast for summer bedding. The plant makes a small bush as wide as it grows tall which is about 9in. It is perennial and readily propagated from cuttings taken in April and inserted into a compost of sand, leaf mould and loam, around the sides of pots. The plant has the appearance of having been painted with the silver paint often used for Christmas decorations, both foliage and stems being completely covered with silver. The stems are rubber-like to the touch.

The plants make a striking contrast when used, possibly two or three to a window box, with the scarlet multiflora begonias, or with scarlet verbena or petunias. The plants should be wintered in a cool or slightly warm greenhouse. Planting out is done early in June, the 60 size pots being inserted into the compost of the window box, or the plants may be removed from the pots. They are re-potted when the boxes are cleared early in October. The plants prefer a soil containing some humus whilst they should not be allowed to lack moisture.

PYRETHRUM PARTHENIUM. **Few know it by its botanical name, for it is Golden Moss or Featherfew, the species** *P. aureum* **having bright golden foliage. Two varieties, one called Golden Ball, which grows to a height of 9in., and Gold Moss, which forms a small compact plant only 4in. high are both ideal for window boxes, while the latter variety could well be used for edging. The featherfews are at their best when used with dark green foliaged plants, whilst they possess an additional charm in the pungency of the foliage.**

It should be given almost the same cultural treatment as that of *Cineraria maritima,* treated as a half-hardy biennial, the seed being sown in cold frames or in a greenhouse during June, pricked off into boxes and again into individual pots, where the plants remain and are wintered in a cold house or closed frame. They should be given a loamy soil, containing a small quantity of peat and grit and will require very little water during winter. The plants are generally set out with the summer window box plants, but are very hardy and could be used any time from early April. Their bright yellow foliage remains colourful right through summer whatever the weather. When purchasing the seed, be sure to obtain the true dwarf Golden Moss strain.

Chapter 10
TRAILING PLANTS

THEIR USE FOR WINDOW BOXES, HANGING BASKETS AND VASES

Preparation of the basket — The vase and its preparation — Climbing plants — Fuchsia — Geranium — Ivy — Lobelia Sapphire — Nasturtium — Nepeta — Pendant Begonia — Petunia — Phlox Drummondii — Tradescantia — Verbena.

Hung suspended from the wall of a courtyard which would otherwise be devoid of colour, or from the eaves of a bungalow where the baskets are low enough to be tended with ease, or even hung around a small garden on stout wires held up by angle-iron stakes, hanging baskets add charm and colour to what may otherwise be drab surroundings. They are so easily made up, and yet, except about hotels and places of public entertainment, they are rarely seen.

The strong wire 'baskets' may be obtained from most large sundries-men. They will, if carefully watered and tended, remain colourful from early summer, say the end of May, until well into autumn. And so that watering may be accomplished without trouble, the baskets should be hung where they may easily be reached. The regular removal of dead flowers, too, will make accessibility an essential.

The baskets are made of strong wire fastened close together which ensures that the compost does not fall through, yet at the same time it allows any excess water to get away. This is very important, for during a warm, dry summer watering may be necessary twice a day, the foliage and blooms also being given a spraying at intervals.

In making up the baskets they should first be lined to a depth of 1in. with new sphagnum moss which will not only restrain the compost from falling through the wires but will help to absorb the moisture. Then place round the sides a layer of new turf, with the soil side to the centre, and carefully mould it to the exact shape of the basket. Then to within 2in. of the top of the basket is placed the prepared compost. This should consist of turf loam to which is added some decayed manure, a sprinkling of lime to keep it sweet, and a little bone meal to provide a constant source of plant food right through the summer.

The plants should be set about the basket from 3in. pots and only those plants with an informal trailing habit should be used, the varieties required being the opposite in habit to most of those used for window boxes. Instead of those of dwarf, compact habit, being planted, certain foliage plants and those of trailing habit are most suitable.

THE VASE AND ITS PREPARATION

The same plants will prove most suitable for garden vases which may also be used on a terrace or verandah, particularly where garden space is at a minimum, and very charming they may be made. Many of these plants, too, may be used for trailing over the sides of a window box and also in an upwards direction. Those who have seen a small window, particularly where leaded panes have been used, surrounded by an elegant climbing plant growing from the ends of a window box, will have seen window box gardening in its most graceful form.

But first the ornamental vases. These were used to great effect by the Victorians and now that our gardening has to be done in more confined conditions, the vogue for using vases is returning. But to be successful, the vase should be at least 12in. deep. A shallow vase will grow little other than the spring flowering plants such as double daisies and primroses, which are shallow rooting, and where confined to the vases only during the less warm and dry periods of the year, do not have to search for moisture. But as vases, like window boxes, are used throughout the year, and will be at their best during summer and autumn, there must be a reasonable depth of soil and this must be prepared with as much care as is given to the compost for a window box or tub.

All too often vases are planted year after year without the soil, often from an old town garden, ever being replenished. Where situated in an industrial city, the compost will soon become of an acid nature due to the constant deposits of soot and sulphur. It should therefore be replaced at least in alternate years. Care must also be taken to make up the compost so that winter and spring flowering plants will receive ample drainage, and summer flowering plants will receive sufficient moisture. Especially is this important where one may be away from home for several weeks at a time.

Drainage is provided by placing crocks at the bottom of the vase to a depth of about 2in. Over this the compost is placed and this should consist of fresh loam which will be free from deposits of soot and sulphur, and to which has been mixed 1oz. of bone meal, some gritty sand and a small quantity of peat or leaf mould. The vase should be filled to the top, but before planting, allow the compost to settle down. After a few days it will be found to have sunk about ½in. below the rim of the vase, which will allow for summer watering without splashing the soil over the sides.

Almost all the plants described as being suitable for window boxes will be equally suitable for a vase, and especially those which grow to a height of between 9in. and 12in. The same use may also be made of a vase in providing a winter and spring display, as well as colour during summer and autumn, though with the average size vase there will not be quite so much scope as with a window box. It must also be remembered that being placed away from the protection of a house, the plants will be subject to more buffeting by strong winds than those growing in a window box.

William Robinson, the great Victorian authority, has suggested that trailing plants, at their best when used in a case or hanging basket, may be left permanently in position planted round the side, for which purpose he suggested the ivies and periwinkles. Against this is the need for providing fresh soil every two or three years, and the fact that in a town garden the foliage will tend to become covered with soot deposits which will spoil the display.

CLIMBING PLANTS

The ivies are certainly most attractive when used either in a vase or when grown from the ends of a window box and trained round a small window. In this way the plants should be planted permanently, and the most satisfactory method is to make two small partitions at either end of the box, allowing sufficient room to accommodate a plant from a 3in. pot. A compost enriched with a little manure should be provided, for with this addition it is surprising how much more vigorous growth will be. The plants may be grown up the wall without any support, in fact only those plants which are able to support themselves should be planted. There is thus no need for any unsightly supports or for damage to the window surrounds. The ivy being evergreen is more suitable than the Virginian Creeper, but in sheltered positions in the south *Campsis Radicans,* also self-clinging and bearing vivid scarlet trumpets in summer, is a glorious sight grown around a window, particularly where the walls are washed. In the south, too, the Passion Flower, *Passiflora caerulea,* may be used to garland a window, but it must be grown up canes which may be held in position by placing at an angle and fastening the top to the wall. Another delightful plant is the remarkable ivy-leaf geranium L'Elegante. It is more like an ivy than a geranium for it makes rapid growth though it requires supporting. It will, however, climb to a height of 4 ft. in a single season. It should be grown permanently in a pot, for it will not survive the winter outdoors. However, if taken indoors it may be used to cover a trellis, or the wall of a room and may be planted outside again in June.

Almost the same plants should be used for a vase as for a hanging basket, for an ornamental vase correctly made, should possess the same light appearance. This means using for both, those plants which are of trailing or semi-trailing habit. The same plants may also be used for trailing over the sides of a window box or tub, and in this instance they will be used chiefly for covering the sides of the containers rather than for their ability to create effect.

These plants are of pendulous or trailing habit:—

FUCHSIA. With their attractive pendulous habit, these make charming plants used in hanging baskets. They may also be used for a large window box, planted with *Cineraria maritima,* with its silver foliage. Some heat, however, will be necessary for their culture, and though they are in no way difficult to manage, they do demand some attention to detail if they are to be grown to perfection. Cuttings are taken from stock plants reserved for the purpose which are grown on in large pots outdoors from June until early September, and from then in a warm greenhouse, the shoots being removed from September until early April. The cuttings, taken when about 2in. long, root readily in a compost of peat and coarse sand, and if sprayed daily to prevent wilting, will be rooted in about three weeks. As the rooting compost will be sterile, the cuttings should be removed to individual pots as soon as well rooted into a compost made up of fibrous loam, decayed manure, together with a small quantity of peat and grit. Fuchsias, unlike begonias, are not lime lovers.

The plants are grown on in a temperature of 55° F to 60° F., as they must not be allowed to grow 'hard', which will cause them to bloom prematurely. But regular syringing and adequate ventilation are necessary and if the spring sun is unduly warm, some shading should be given to prevent leaf scorch. Those plants struck before Christmas will require a second move to larger pots in early March to keep them growing, and when 8in. to 9in. high should have their shoots pinched back to encourage bushy growth. From early April the plants should be fed with liquid manure water and should be moved to frames for hardening in mid-May.

The plants will be ready for the baskets early in June and they should be planted as an alternative to the geranium rather than with them, for unlike the geraniums they require considerable moisture, otherwise they will drop their blooms during a hot period.

There are many outstanding varieties, but for planting together, Ballet Girl, with its red sepals and double white corolla, is most attractive. So is the all-pink coloured Fascination, also a double, and the rose and purple Profusion. All of these varieties are easy to grow, are tolerant of wet weather and are free flowering bedding plants.

GERANIUM. It is the ivy-leaf varieties with their semi-trailing habit which are so useful for ornamental vases, boxes and hanging baskets. They are ideal plants, not only for their pretty pale green foliage and great freedom of blooming, but for their ability to withstand dry conditions. They are at their best used with marguerites, with their light, feathery habit, and with the variegated tradescantia or nepeta with their long trailing habit. For their description and culture see Chapter 6.

The variety L'Elegante should receive special mention here, for it is almost of climbing habit, but may be used equally well for trailing from a basket or vase. Its bottle-green leaves, edged with cream are most colourful, whilst it provides a pleasing contrast to the paler green leaves of the flowering ivy-leaf varieties. L'Elegante bears only inconspicuous mauve-pink flowers and should be planted entirely for its foliage and habit. Early in October the plants should be taken indoors where they may be used to trail over a wall or trellis or along a window ledge. They will require almost no water during winter and any unduly long shoots may be pinched back and the cuttings rooted in pots of sandy soil kept almost dry.

IVY. Happy in the smoke-laden atmosphere of a town, the variegated ivies are valuable plants for a vase or window box. They should be grown in 3in. pots, for they resent root disturbance. They may be planted in autumn to provide winter colour and as William Robinson suggested, they may be left permanently in position. For summer display, however, they should be replaced by ivy-leaf geraniums, or annuals of trailing habit, unless it be that the plants can be given little attention, when they should be made permanent.

Perhaps even more attractive are the ivies when used to garland a window as described, but make certain that only the small leaved varieties are used, of which Silver Queen with its small, neat leaves, attractively edged with silver is the best.

LOBELIA SAPPHIRE. This is the only trailing lobelia. Its blooms, borne in cascade fashion, are a deep sapphire-blue colour with an attractive white eye. Like the verbenas, it may be propagated from cuttings inserted in sandy soil in October, or from seed sown in heat in January, pricking off the seedlings and growing on in a warm greenhouse. The plants should be used in the centre of a basket so that the cascade of bloom is seen to advantage.

NASTURTIUM. The best variety for hanging baskets is a fully double salmon-red, propagated only by rooting the cuttings in sandy soil in September. For best results transplant into 2½in. pots in November. The plants have a trailing habit and bloom profusely, and should be planted round the sides of a basket.

The double Gleam Hybrids are also very beautiful and if allowed to grow away without any stopping, make an excellent display with their vivid scarlet, salmon, gold and yellow blooms which are larger but perhaps not so dainty in formation as the double salmon-red form described above.

NEPETA. It is not the common form of nepeta or catmint used for edging a border that is used for its trailing habit, but the trailing, variegated leaf form. The best way of increasing stock is to plant several plants in a bed of oil where during summer they will send out their long strawbery-like runners and will take root at the leaf joints in a similar way. The individual plants may then be lifted and potted and grown on in a cold frame for using in baskets, vases or tubs. Being quite hardy, planting may take place at any time, the small cream and green leaves giving an appearance of considerable lightness.

PENDANT BEGONIAS. This is a most attractive type of the begonia species, similar in habit to the more common double tuberous type but it has a free branching habit and single flowers very freely produced. A temperature of 55°F. is necessary to start the tubers into growth, and for this reason it is essential to possess a heated house though when only a small number of plants are required the tubers may be started into growth in a warm, light position in the dwelling house. The tubers will give quite good results if planted in the dormant state directly into the basket in early April, though of course the display of bloom would be later. Normally, the tubers will be started into growth in single 2½in. pots in a warm house in early February, and given the necessary moisture requirements and a suitable compost containing plenty of either leaf mould or peat. By the middle of April they will have become sturdy plants, and they may then be knocked from the pots and planted firmly into the prepared basket. Begonias greatly enjoy a once weekly watering with weak liquid cow manure and at all times during the summer must be given quite heavy regular waterings. They will come into bloom in June and remain a mass of colour until early October when the baskets should be taken indoors to prevent damage by frost. When the other plants have been removed, the begonias should be allowed to die down by withholding water. They may then be removed and stored in a dry place until required again early next year.

Lovely varieties are Broadacre, deepest rose-pink; Alice Manning, rich yellow; Joan, coral-pink; and Sunset, orange-salmon.

PETUNIA. Though they cannot be classed as trailing plants, the taller, long-jointed members of the colourful petunia family are valuable plants for a hanging basket, planted as an alternative to geraniums. The plants may only be raised in heat or purchased from a nurseryman.

Outstanding varieties are General Dodds, crimson; Inimitable, white, striped crimson; Blue Bee, violet blue; and Rose King, with its attractive white throat.

PHLOX DRUMMONDII. Whilst the *nana compacta* varieties are now used entirely for bedding and for window box culture, the older grandiflora varieties make excellent vase and basket plants with their loose, semi-trailing habit. They make up a charming vase display, planted with Sapphire lobelia and the ivy-leaf geraniums. Use a pink geranium with Cinnebar-scarlet phlox, or use crimson and white geraniums with rose-pink phlox, Brilliant, and allow Sapphire lobelia to trail over the sides.

TRADESCANTIA. The trailing variegated-leaf *Tradescantia fluminensis,* so often seen growing as an indoor pot plant, may successfully be used for hanging baskets and window boxes during summer. Like L'Elegante geranium, the plants should be taken indoors in October when they will continue to remain colourful throughout the winter. The silver leaves are striped with green and mauve making a most colourful display when planted with scarlet ivy-leaf geraniums, especially the vivid scarlet double flowered Mrs. W. A. R. Clifton. Propagation is from cuttings taken at almost any time of the year. They will root readily in a sandy compost round the side of a pot in a room window. The geraniums may also be rooted in a similar way and so both plants may be used together where neither garden nor greenhouse is available.

VERBENA. Whilst the more compact varieties will be used for window box display, those of more trailing habit are most attractive when used in vases and hanging baskets. The plants should be raised in a warm greenhouse either from cuttings taken in September, or from seed sown early in January. Cuttings may be wintered in a window of a living room if placed in a sandy compost and kept almost dry. They will have made sturdy plants to be planted in the baskets early in June. One of the most striking varieties is Etna, vivid scarlet with a golden eye; but where a softer shade is required, Ellen Wilmott, salmon-pink, and Lavender Glory are excellent. As a contrast to the more brilliant colours, Snow Queen with its pure-white heads, is a valuable variety.